GREAT HUNTING ADVENTURES

VOLUME 3

Henry E. Prante

Great Hunting Adventures
Volume 3
Henry E. Prante
Copyright © 2020 by Hella Prante

All rights reserved. No part of this book may be used or reproduced in any manner whatsoever without written permission except in the case of brief quotations embodied in critical articles or reviews.

This book is true to the best of my recollections. Some of the names, businesses, events and incidents have been changed to protect the identity of these persons.

For information

Contact: HellaPrante@gmail,com
Book Design: Hella Prante
First Edition: December 2020
10 9 8 7 6 5 4 3 2 1

DEDICATED TO:

BRIGITTE PRANTE: Our loving Mother, Grandmother & Wife who has dealt with so much in this lifetime including being a "hunting" widow.

OTHER BOOKS

PRINT Books

Great Hunting Adventures Volume 1 & 2 &3

3 SIMPLE WOODWORKING PROJECTS: In the Workshop with Henry

KINDLE eBooks

Great Hunting Adventures Volume 1 & 2 & 3

3 SIMPLE WOODWORKING PROJECTS: In the Workshop with Henry

17 Easy Steps to Build Your Own Portable "Camp Kitchen": In the Workshop With Henry Series ("In the Workshop with Henry

21 Easy Steps to Build Your Complete Gun & Ammo "Compact" Case: In the Workshop With Henry Series

49 Easy Steps to Build Your Own "Marsh Fox" Duck Punt: "In the Workshop with Henry" Series

9 Easy Steps to Build Your Own Port-O-Kennel: In the Workshop with Henry Series

British Columbia's "River of No Return": The Coquitlam River

Fibreglass Is Everybody's Friend: Even the repairman's…sometimes…

www.greathuntingadventures.com

DEDICATED TO:	i
OTHER BOOKS	iii
SUNDAY HUNTERS	1
THE BEST TIME FOR BEAR HUNTING	9
FAST AND FURIOUS	25
GREEN HILLS AND SWEET STEAKS	30
HUNTING THE ROCKY MOUNTAIN GOAT	39
"WILD ANIMALS — WHAT WILL THEY DO NEXT?"	54
SHEEP HUNTING ANYONE?	64
THE STORY OF LUCKY	78
SURVIVING IN STYLE	86
STUCK IN THE MUD MOOSE	93
THE IDEAL DUCK PUNT MEANS BETTER HUNTING	106
THE ART OF TRACKING GAME	115
THE DAY THE WOLVES HOWLED	125
HUNTING DIARY (excerpt)	132
The Call of the Wild	138
The Cremation of Sam McGee	141
PHOTOS	146

SUNDAY HUNTERS

TO BE CALLED A 'SUNDAY HUNTER' is never regarded as a great compliment by aspiring nimrods. Of course there are some very good reasons why this is so, but most hunters would much rather fly off the proverbial handle than ponder why this term has ever come into use.

"Sure I know what it means," snorted a good friend of mine when I used that tag on him in jest. "You think I am stupid and don't know what I'm doing huh?"

I figure he added the questioning "huh?" because he hoped I would apologize for the insult.

Well strange as it may seem, until that long past day I had never given this term any particular thought. After all don't most of our hunters attempt the fair chase on weekends, if only for lack of other free time? That is how I did it once upon a time.

Surely herein lies the root of the imagined slander, because far too many weekend experts fit neatly into the 'Sunday Hunter' category, including even a fair number of folk who are paid by the taxpayer to manage our wildlife on a full-time basis. Perhaps you can see some justice in this fact – as the saying goes – "It might indeed require an ass to work with jackasses, eh?"

It is no state secret that the vast majority of our hunters are enthusiastic amateurs who have the burning desire… but little realistic chance to catch up with any 'big game', British Columbia animal until they have served a rather costly apprenticeship. Few aspiring nimrods will believe this at first. But they will … once they have followed many miles of cold trails, empty tracks and have learned first-hand what hunting any specific game animal is all about… or until they have hired a very competent guide to help out.

I must confess that I can remember many unsuccessful, albeit happy hunts for deer, elk, moose, mountain goats, grizzly bears, and bighorn sheep. It became frightening at times. Breathtaking... and even dangerous during others. I became much more successful once I forgot about weekend hunting, and organized much longer hunting trips that lead me ever further afield. Over time I found this was a much safer and more enjoyable arrangement as well.

I will never forget one elk hunt because it was also the first time I actually had to dodge bullets from fellow hunters. I was near Princeton, BC. on the last day of the hunting season nearly 50 years ago. It was a cold, snowy November morning, and I had camped inside my "pulmanized" car just off the main highway. I awakened to gunfire that might have indicated a minor outbreak of war and the whistling sounds of rifle bullets.

I was surrounded by hunters who were blasting away at something near me. I left my vehicle rather quickly taking along my rifle and some ammunition and hid in a nearby bush. I seriously thought I might have to defend myself before the shooting finally stopped. A few minutes later two elk came running past the bush I was using for cover and I shot one of them. Later I learned that a whole herd of elk had been killed that morning in the area I was in.

The following year I spent almost every weekend in the same territory without much success. One morning a partner and I heard some nearby shooting and decided to investigate the cause. We found three middle aged hunters had killed a five-point, bull elk.

The problem was – the elk season hadn't yet begun. Being surprised and spooked by us, the hunters acted cagy. Not knowing who we were, and they were old-timers' at this game compared to us kids – they decided to bluff their way out of their dilemma.

"Hey, boys! Have you ever seen such a big mule deer buck before?"

We had planned just to go past them when one of them involved us into a conversation. My partner was quick to catch on.

"Wow!" he hollered.

"Can't say I have. That sure is a beaut! Any more like that around here? I sure would like to get one too!"

The poachers pointed up a side hill. "In there! There was a whole herd of 'em over there, Why don't you fellows go of after 'em?"

"Great idea!" my partner drooled. "Thanks for telling us."

Turning toward me he suggested: "Come on! Let's get' em! What are you waiting for?"

While the poachers snickered we made our exit from the scene of their crimes rather rapidly.

"Quick thinking, old man!" I said once we were at a safe distance.

"Let them think we're stupid."

"Sure," he replied. "I don't want to get murdered for being an unwelcome witness. Where I come from poachers don't like to leave witnesses alive telling tales on 'em."

Since both of us had grown up in central Europe where many a gamekeeper has been murdered by poachers, I knew what he meant. Pretending to be stupid was a reasonable price to pay. We were miffed too. We had expected to find at least a genuine mule deer buck in that meadow… and the following day we might have been able to bag that bull elk legally.

In the following years we hunted that same meadow often... even on horseback and never saw another good bull elk within shooting range. I bagged some fine mule deer bucks there, a bear and many grouse. I had never seen a better hunting country. However, with the benefit of hindsight, I don't believe I will hunt this area again, although I still like to trail ride there on occasion. I simply find that most modern hunters are in too great a hurry to kill something– anything– and this leaves me feeling unsafe and uncomfortable in heavily hunted areas.

The ancient urge to kill and provide is still alive and well in modern man although many of them will deny it. It is a very powerful urge and when misguided, or unbridled, or just plain misunderstood. It can become the root of trouble for our society. One can safely assume that every human being, given the opportunity under specific circumstances, is still capable of killing. The daily press and media often reports in gruesome detail just how misguided 'killing' is often practiced.

It always amazes me how people can froth at the mouth in protest over the legal killing of wild game and yet practice their own brand of murderous politics or business. It is lamentable that not all monkeys live in the safe confinement of a zoo. It is even more pitiful that many are allowed to occupy high and fancy offices – alas still unable to understand even the most primitive and basic facts of life that ought to govern human behavior.

I believe today's 'Sunday Hunter' has acquired a poor reputation by acting in a thoughtless manner and showing a lack of due consideration for the rights of others. Many years ago when I extended my own hunting territory far afield I began to understand why people disliked the Sunday-variety of hunters so much. I couldn't help but notice that wilderness accommodation such as cabins and camps within a short weekend's driving distance of the big city were usually ransacked, wrecked or totally destroyed by gun-toting jerks.

For the longest time I couldn't accept or believe that hunters would be so destructive. Yet I saw the bullet holes in the wreckage, and parts of killed game littering the campsites. It was puzzling due to the fact in remote regions, far from population centers, such wilderness accommodation was usually intact and quite serviceable.

In the East Kootenay's I found many such cabins with serviceable heaters and furnishings that were unlocked and open to whoever needed to use them. These were greatly appreciated. I would occasionally find a little graffiti writing on the walls, but usually these wilderness shelters were quite serviceable. But, within weekend driving distance of the large cities I would only find much trash and ruins that were shot full of holes.

Of course, it is always hard to point an accusing finger, but it is more than just reasonable to assume that jerks who had no personal need for accommodation were the culprits. This, of course, points the finger at the self-contained, travelling 'Sunday Hunter'.

These people had never planned to use existing accommodation – nor stay anywhere long enough to need it. Reason leads me to believe that no one will deliberately wreck good accommodation if he, or she, will likely still need it.

Even in the far North of British Columbia, the times seems to have changed human behavior. Where once I found great accommodation in old mining camps, these days one finds little more than garbage these days.

The only decent cabins I have seen in the north are the highway department's emergency shelters on the road to Atlin, B.C. Out in the wilderness, where no owner is present or presumed to exist – destruction is sure to follow. Of course the general public blames the "damn hunters" and we will forever live with the accusations.

Last September I revisited a favorite hunting area in the North Country, where I have spent many happy days of camping, hunting and fishing. Every year for fifteen seasons I have kept the place clean and free of garbage. On many occasions I first had to clean it up before I could stay there. In some years, I was the first hunter of the season to camp there and yet the place was a mess.

This leads me to believe that many folks must be as disorderly as some hunters are. It was interesting to observe that many of the piles of garbage left behind by gold-digging miners have been over-valued these days – but the much smaller heaps left by an untidy hunter can easily be treated as a "crime" of national importance.

On one occasion I found some personal papers belonging to a police officer. When I took that garbage bag to the man's commanding officer... all hell broke loose. I was asked if I really believed that I could get away with such accusation.

Well to make a long story short— I did and the litterbug was transferred clean out of the province – before he could have a fair trial. I cannot tell for sure if he was just a 'Sunday Hunter', a bird watcher, or fisherman. To tell the whole truth and nothing but – I couldn't care less if he had been a charter member of Green Peace or any other environmental group. A clean B.C. is much more enjoyable for all.

THE BEST TIME FOR BEAR HUNTING

March 6, 1985

"WHY WOULD YOU GO HUNTING in the spring? I mean – what can you possibly hunt in May?"

Almost every year I am asked these questions, usually by someone who has no concept about bears and hunting.

"I have some very good reasons," I usually respond.

"For me it is too damn long to wait until September for openers. The bear season is open around the first week of April and considering that a bears hide – in the spring of the year – is usually of much better quality than during the early fall season. Besides, in the fall I prefer to hunt for venison and I haven't time to bother with bears – unless of course they managed to get on the wrong side of me – or I want a fat bear for his lard and meat."

After the long winter I am usually chomping at the bit to get into the field early. I usually hunt in very different areas than those where my venison comes from. But my greatest concern with bear hunting is the quality of their hides. I find it simply unforgivable to kill a bear for a hide that when tanned lays as flat as a postage stamp without the luxurious winter wool between the hair. The meat will usually be good to eat.

In the southern portions of British Columbia a good bear hide is hard to find before their normal hibernation time at the end of the regular hunting season – unless it is in the spring. The weather is usually too mild for far too long to cause Mr. Bruin to grow heavy wool. In the northern regions of the province it is quite different.

One day while hunting caribou above the timberline of a far northern mountain, I ran head-on into a hog-fat bear with awesome fur. We both surprised each other at about 10 feet apart. The bear stood up and got his hackles up until he looked about twice as tall as he really was. He rattled his teeth similar to a human who is freezing in a snowstorm. A deep throaty growl came from the depths of his chest and this spectre made my hair raise my hat a couple of inches.

I instantly realized that one lightning-fast jump would land the indignant bear right on top of me sending me to the happy hunting grounds. The bear hesitated. My quickly snapped shot between his little pig eyes settled that argument before I could lose it. This bear had a beautiful, fine and silky fur coat. While I had no intentions of killing a bear that day I decided to make the best of the situation by utilizing the whole animal. I packed the whole carcass to my campsite.

I had already been out in the bush for two weeks. The weather had been windy and freezing cold. My hands showed deep skin cracks that were sore as hell. The next morning, after I had skinned the fat animal, I was pleasantly surprised by the condition of my hands. The bleeding cracks no longer hurt.

I recall that while skinning the bear, my nose had itched and I had rubbed it – and even the cold sores were beginning to heal. I deduced that bear fat had some medicinal properties indeed so I rendered a large pot full of fat just this purpose. I don't know if the bear grease made me smell very good – but it sure healed up all my sores much quicker than it normally would have taken.

Furthermore, I found that the bear grease will soak right through leather. Later, once home again, I melted some beeswax and mixed it with bear grease – and it really worked well to keep my leather boots waterproofed.

The finished bear rug was a luxurious thing indeed. It was quite expensive to have it tanned and blocked but it was definitely worth the cost. It became a floor mat beside my bed, and remained a perfect reminder of a dangerous encounter.

In British Columbia, it seems, we have an abundance of black bears. This is especially true of the southern half of the province and specifically in and around the suburbs of Vancouver. The bear populations in recent years have grown rapidly, and in too many areas they are killed as dangerous vermin, because live trapping and transportation to faraway regions are more expensive alternatives, and do not work as well as some folks believe.

Since I love to hunt and get away from suburbia – from a life that seems to become more hysterical with each passing year – bear hunting gives me the perfect opportunity. Even at that time the bugs and mosquitoes are out in full force – but still – that quiet hunt through a budding forest – the sweet scents of new young growth in my nostrils compensate for all of that.

In the spring the visibility in the bush is far greater as well. Another reason that bears can be more easily found in the spring is that these great opportunists roam far and wide in their search for sustenance. You can usually find them in mountain meadows or at the foot of avalanche tracks where they can be seen from a distance.

In contrast, in the fall, bear hunts should be hunted with trained dogs to be successful. And – still the hunter can be in for some very unpleasant surprises just as I mentioned previously.

I have studied too many bears to take such hunting lightly. Even a yearling black bear is already too big and strong to tangle with. He can kill a grown man if he decides to do so. I recall that an acquaintance of mine once tried to capture two little cubs who seemed to have lost her mother. Before he got those little rascals out of the tree they had climbed – he looked as though a horse had dragged him through a couple miles of blackberry brambles.

When skinning a bear, take a close look at the powerful muscles, even Arnold Schwarzenegger would be jealous of those biceps.

My first meeting with a black bear came about on a cool October evening on a logging road high above Emory Creek, in the Fraser Canyon. My partner and I had hunted for deer and we were walking back towards the car when suddenly my partner fired a lightning-quick shot. We had been walking side-by-side at the time – and carrying on our conversation and not particularly quietly.

"What in hell was that for?" I gasped in total surprise.

"Bear!" He shouted.

But I hadn't seen the bear and said as much.

"He was on the road, right at that curve, no more than 30 yards in front of us!"

I couldn't believe it, but readied my rifle anyway. The landscape surrounding us was fairly level, but full of huge stumps and thick underbrush.

"Did you hit him?" I asked.

"Dunno," he replied as he headed for the spot where he had last seen the bear.

We were both relatively green in the hunting game at that time, and I was somewhat nervous about bears as well.

"Weren't bear supposed to be highly dangerous, especially if wounded?" I asked myself while craning my neck to see if I could spot the bear before he could come for me.

Not so my partner. He plunged head-on into the thickets. I don't really know why I spotted the movement at all in that green bush – but 50 yards away – over the butt end of a huge log I saw the bear poke his head out. He was watching my partner. In order to see better he stood up and showed his chest.

My partner had no chance of seeing the bear from where he was. I raised my rifle and brought the site to the center of the bear's chest and fired. The bear dropped instantly, but within a second he began the most unnerving bawling. He sounded like a poor lost sheep.

"You hit him hard," my partner yelled.

"Let's get over there and put him out of that misery!"

I still urged caution. But he wanted none of that.

"Let's make the poor bugger stop this infernal racket."

Rifles at the ready – we advanced. It wasn't easy to cover the distance. When I finally climbed on top of that log, I could see the bear down, but still flailing his paws like the wings of a windmill.

Just as I was about to dispatch him my partner yelled "No! Hold it!"

There was a lot of blood splattered about but I could see a large hole in the bear's chest.

"You'll just blow another big hole in that fine pelt," he argued.

"Here," he drew his knife.

"I'll finish them off with this." Without further ado he jumped onto the bear's back, grabbed him by the scruff of the neck, and stabbed him in the throat. For a brief moment he sliced away as if he were cutting bread. Suddenly – the bear was quiet and lay still.

I shuddered. I could feel beads of hot sweat dripping off my brow and I wasn't very steady on my feet either.

"Why... did... you... d-d-d-do that?" I stuttered.

"I-co-co-co-could've shot-him-again."

"Yeah, I know," he replied while wiping his blade on some grass.

He rolled the bear onto his back, "but look here – I didn't really want you to blow another big hole into this great hide. That would've ruined everything."

Consequent examination of the bullet wound showed that my bullet had hit the breast bone – exploded into a shower of shrapnel – and tore a huge hole. Bullet splinters had even destroyed the bear's lungs and entered his heart. Needless to say I came away with much respect for 30-06 hunting ammunition and the damage it can do.

Of course I won't ever forget that first bear encounter, or the foolhardiness my partner displayed jumping right onto that bear. The bear was not too large, 300 pounds perhaps. But, he could've been quite a handful under only slightly different circumstances. He was a boar and as fat as a Thanksgiving turkey. His hide was not so ruined that we couldn't use it – but definitely didn't compare to most spring bears I have since bagged and continue to hunt.

The third fall bear I killed was a grizzly who just happened to hunt moose. He figured since I was in his way, I wouldn't be an insurmountable obstacle. He seemed like he wanted to run right over me. But, this was his fatal mistake. Two shots dropped that bear stone dead, but while it lasted – that silvertip boar created more excitement than I thought I could stand.

The last thing a hunter needs is to stumble up onto a bear at close range. It doesn't really matter what species of bear, because even black bears have been known to attack and fight. If you surprise a bear you had better have a clean field of fire.

One fine Victoria Day weekend in May, my partners and I trudged along the old logging road that used to lead from Bralorne, B.C. through to the Hurley River Pass towards Pemberton. The road wasn't completed yet, so this area of the country was actually very remote, but famous for its grizzlies.

It was a hot day as well. Melt-water bubbled and gurgled everywhere in thousands of rivulets off the snowfields and avalanche slides of the greening mountains. We saw plenty of bear spoor on the road and many so-called bear trees that showed claw and bite marks.

My partners were a few steps behind me, when suddenly an adult black bear who had apparently just come off the mountainside, popped onto the road a scant 50 yards in front of me. I happened to carry my rifle in my hand at the time and raised my gun and fired at his chest. But the bear had seen me too.

My bullets spun him completely around, but he made the effort of trying to run and he got off the road. There was a lot of blood on the ground, and when I looked up again, I saw him dragging himself through some willow bushes. Not one to play with knives unnecessarily like my other partner, I fired again and he lay still.

My partners came running. We advanced on the dead bear with caution. Joe Ringwald wanted to circle the animal, and as he walked past a few Christmas trees, I spotted a movement under a tree no more than a few steps from Joe.

I yelled for him to watch out. Instantly a large chocolate- colored bear streaked out of his cover and vanished into some bushes a little further away. Joe nearly jumped out of his boots in surprise.

To him, it seemed he had almost stepped onto that bears' tail and he never got to shoot. Both he and my other partner, Frank Kasa, then set out to hunt for the brown bear while I had the job of skinning out my black one.

I might confess that knowing my bear had a traveling companion and this companion might be a calculating devil – I looked over my shoulders an awful lot. The natural sounds of bear country in spring can be very distracting. Squirrels are rustling in the old dry leaves. Birds are flitting through the shrubbery and everywhere there is the sound of rushing water. I was quite pleased when my friends came back, even though they hadn't found the other bear.

The moist spring ground muffles the sound of footsteps, so both bear and hunter can be surprised when they fail to hear approaching steps. So it was on the following day, near the Cadwallader River, when Joe surprised another bear under similar circumstances among the willows and alders of an avalanche track. The difference here is that Joe Ringwald had seen the bear from a distance, and this bear never knew what killed it.

One of the handsomest bears I have ever seen was a large, reddish blond boar who stood near a logging road looking at us when I was hunting with Henry Gebauer, of Gold Bridge, B.C. and Frank Kasa. Previously I had scouted for bears in the general vicinity of Gold Bridge but found none.

It was evening, towards the end of May. Henry stopped his truck, but when I stepped out to load my rifle – Mr. Bruin disappeared fast. I was disappointed, but we drove on. Two miles further down the road we spotted another bear digging in a pile of rotting logs. Frank bagged that coal-black bear.

The following morning Frank and I drove back to where "Blondie" had been. I parked the truck, and we set out on foot to hunt for him. We were only 20 paces from the truck when Frank pointed to our left.

"There he is!"

About 200 yards away, he was feeding like a contented cow on the new grasses and dandelions. This was a one-shot kill. It was only 6:50 AM.

I found my 180 grain 30-06 Silvertip bullet had broken both of the bear's shoulders and he was dead when we reached him. Thick wool still covered his heavy body. He was one fine bear.

We skinned him on the spot and took his edible meat with us when we returned home. A friend who owned a butcher shop and delicatessen salted and smoked the hams using old Westphalian ham recipes and spices. This meat was delicious.

Later, when we returned to Henry Gebauer's abode, to show off my prize, he just grinned.

"So, you think you've done pretty good, eh?"

'Wait until you see what I have."

From the depths of his home freezer he produced a bundle of black fur – another bear. This critter had attempted to break into Henry's chicken coop while he had his after lunch siesta. His wife heard the commotion in the backyard – looked out of the window – and spotted the troublemaker. Right from the kitchen window – she shot that bear.

During our one-week stay we saw 11 bears and all had good fur. Frank even saw a black bear sow with two cubs and I saw a grizzly. The way Frank told of his experience, he considered himself lucky that the sow didn't attempt to run him over.

In over 30 years of hunting; if my memory serves me correctly; I have killed over a dozen bears. I wouldn't consider myself an expert on that subject, because every bear encounter is different. Perhaps I was just luckier than some bear hunters are.

One thing I have learned about them, though, is that Mr. and Mrs. Bruin deserves respect. I have never killed one for sport, and I take a few liberties, or chances with them. Bears are too powerful to play with, and they can be very dangerous. But, they are always exciting to hunt.

The true wilderness bear, the one that isn't spoiled rotten by tourists and garbage, is always the hardest to hunt. Usually he manages to get away clean.

Every now and then one reads some so-called expert's advice column on how to behave in bear country. It is all well intended of course, but somehow those "helpful hints" can be an awful pain, or totally impractical.

Imagine for a moment an ordinary pet dog whose hearing is so keen that he can detect the pussycat next door walking outside the house on a cement walkway while your radio is playing inside at the same time. My own dog, Fritz demonstrated this ability to me one evening, and ever since he has become my hunting partner.

The advice givers usually claim a hiker in the woods, in bear country, should make a lot of noise and this noise will scare bears away. They also often claim one ought not to keep food with you or you are inviting a bear to come to it.

This theory may be right enough, but where on earth is a backpacking hunter in the high country going to keep his supplies? There are no trees above the timberline upon which to hang a food box.

As for making noise, I would seriously consider why anyone would hike in the wilderness without real protection. Is it to enjoy solitude, nature, peace and quiet, to view wildlife, or to scare everything away?

Bears are rather curious animals and may well lay in wait to see what is coming up the trail. For many years I have kept my moose meat close to camp, where I can see it, and protect it from marauding bears. I recall one northern trip when six hunting parties had a dozen moose hanging from the meat poles within a 100 yard radius. This was in excellent grizzly country as well, but we never had any bear trouble. Two other hunters a quarter-mile away who hung their moose in one piece 100 yards from their camp – lost the whole thing to a big grizzly.

These days I hunt with my good dog, Fritz, who is very protective, but does not hunt alone. I doubt that a bear could sneak up on us with such an early warning system in place, I feel fairly safe in any bear country. I suppose if the bear charges and really means business, the best policy is always to break their big bones. A big game guide friend of mine claims it works very well.

"So what if he's not instantly dead. Busted shoulders usually slow them down enough to give you another opportunity to reload and fire. Of course, at very close range this can be a rather hair-straightening experience – especially for the novice hunter. "

He continued, "Usually you only have enough time for a quick shot, and that had better be a good one. Repeating a bolt action rifle takes about a second. But during that second Mr. Bruin can travel 25 yards or better. Under these circumstances it is probably best to stand one's ground, and wait with your one shot you have, until it is practically impossible to miss. But – if you do miss, you will just likely have to kiss your ass goodbye!"

A very gutsy and agile dog is probably the best insurance against their attacks and surprises. I happen to trust my German Shepherd to do a great job for me although an Airedale is probably a better choice. Airedale's are smaller, intelligent, and very courageous. They are small enough to fit into a bush plane and are no hazard in a canoe. They are not heavy eaters and are easily cared for. I once watched how a little Airedale drove a big bear up the tallest tree he could find.

Yet, it surprises me just how tough and fast a large German shepherd can be when he has to be. I don't actually hunt bears with my dog because that in and of itself can be a more strenuous exercise than I prefer. Given a choice I'd rather still hunt or sit on the stand and wait for a very sure shot.

To estimate the size of a bear at a distance can be tricky. I recall one occasion when a partner and I thought we saw grizzly on a mountainside. We saw it all through my spotting scope of 60 X. magnification. When we finally arrived in what we thought was a good shooting range... after we had walked an hour to get there... our huge grizzly turned out to be nothing more than a large porcupine.

A small bear at close range can often look much bigger than he really is. Actually in real life a young bear appears quite leggy. The really good sized bear is actually a chunky fellow who almost drags his belly over sticks and stones. He appears to have very short legs. The average weight of an adult black bear is probably no more than 300 pounds. Most are smaller and only the exceptional bear grows larger. Grizzlies are of course a different species, and their weight may go as high as 600-800 pounds. One cannot really mistake the one for the other except in the dark – and your mistake can be quite fatal.

It always amazes me how some folks have the impression that a brown colored bear is always a different species than the black colored one. The truth is, of course, that the common black bear can be found in any color from a creamy white to a stove-pipe black. The grizzly is usually brownish... but may be as platinum blonde as Marilyn Monroe used to be, or nearly as black as coal. Black bear or grizzly, it doesn't pay anyone dividends to fool with either of them.

Once I accidentally walked head on into a large grizzly while hunting moose. He was partially screened by the bush. Fortunately for both of us we kept our tempers to ourselves. We both lived through that experience unscathed. As I have said before – the hunter must be discriminating in the selection of his bear. He must certainly know when it is not necessary to shoot.

FAST AND FURIOUS

1986 BC outdoors

WOLVERINES CAN BE FOUND in most parts of BC and have a justifiable reputation for their ferocity, fearlessness and their surprising strength.

    The late summer afternoon sun was warm and beating down on the surrounding mountains ablaze in brilliant colors, as I sat on the Western slope of Marble Dome Mountain glassing the range for caribou. To my right, a cow and calf browsed through the scrub birch and shintangle that covered the hill in great patches. It was a peaceful scene. Ptarmigan cackled everywhere and a colony of ground squirrels was busy in the scrub behind me.

Suddenly, uphill behind me I heard a blood curdling, throaty growl. I almost jumped out of my boots as I turned around. My rifle was ready to fire but I saw no animal large or dangerous enough to threaten me. At first I thought of my partner, and that he was having some fun with me, but he was nowhere to be seen.

Again that awful growl rang out. It came from close quarters, seemingly from a clump of knee-high scrub the housed a gopher colony. I was confused. No gopher I knew had ever made these menacing sounds before. It must be a bigger beast – a grizzly perhaps? But there was no grizzly, not even a mad black bear.

A blurred movement among the bushes caught my eye. It was just another gopher after all, I surmised. Finally the form of a wolverine became visible. It came straight for me still growling and slavering. This beast closed the distance between us very rapidly. Its tiny black button eyes were fixed upon me. I was to be its next feast or something.

I actually thought it was laughable at first. This animal was no larger than a cocker spaniel. I was armed for much larger game. My hand held my old-school Mauser .30-06 with 180 grain bullets. These are loads capable of killing the largest carnivores on this continent. For all practical purposes, I was Goliath and had the damn slingshot to boot. I felt over gunned and foolish as I was squinted through the 4X telescope. Since I had never contemplated eating wolverine, I never considered killing one.

This beast kept growling and loping toward me and there wasn't much time to think. I was surprised by all the thoughts that raced through my mind. Wolverines are the largest members of the weasel family. They are gutsy and bloodthirsty devils. They are crafty too.

I suddenly recalled how a common weasel once attacked me. To get at me, it had to jump up waist high. I was on my way to work that day and carried only a briefcase which I used to slap at the little monster. I hit it hard three or four times but it kept coming for more. Finally a hard slap dazed the animal, and I threw my briefcase on top of it and jumped on it. This did the trick but I ruined a perfectly good briefcase in the process.

Closer to hand now, I thought of taking the beast in its gleaming chops. Then I might pick it up by the tail and bashes head against a rock. But was this wolverine rabid? Judging by its size, raised hackles and all, it could do a little more damage than my getting a few scratches or a bite before I might simply overpower it. Maybe and maybe not.

It occurred to me I couldn't afford to take foolish chances. I had flown into this remote area and the return plane was not due for another two weeks. I thought of possible blood poisoning. Finally at 10 paces I bent my shooting finger. A heavy rifle boomed as the bullets slammed this wolverine against the ground. But my thoughts were also concerned with the quality of the pelt. I didn't want to ruin it.

Normally, a big game cartridge is capable of blowing big holes into big bodies and hides –- so big in fact that the hides become useless. As luck would have it, after aiming between these hungry eyes, the bullet struck the beast in the wide-open, drooling mouth, blowing away its lower jaw.

But the animal was not yet dead. To prevent further pelt destruction I picked up a fair sized rock meaning to clobber the wolverine on the head with it. I was sure it could no longer bite me now – but was not prepared for its next reaction.

Just as I bent down to hit it with the rock it jumps straight for my face. Perhaps it was still groggy from the shot and because my aim was bad. It sailed right over my left shoulder without touching me. I dropped the rock, aimed the rifle one more time, at the beast's head and fired. This time the bullet hit it instantly and left only a small hole in the fur because it exited where her jaw was already missing.

I was both sad and glad. Sad to have been forced to kill this animal for which I had no particular need or use. Yet glad I didn't miss when it counted most. It was a female but her pelt was not in prime condition. I skinned it anyway and later had it tanned. Today it serves to remind me of what can happen in the wilderness when you least expect it… and how quickly it can happen… and, lastly never to take unnecessary risks.

Wolverines inhabit most areas of our province and you can stumble onto this fearless creature almost anywhere, particularly in rocky alpine areas that contain good populations of ground squirrels, marmot's and the like. They will eat most anything. Their strength is legendary and out of proportion with their size. Their average weight is approximately 22 pounds (10 kilo).

I have seen more wolverines, always in timberline country, but they either didn't spot me or were more peaceful than this one.

Once, however I saw a grizzly bear and a wolverine meet on a trail. I was surprised to see the bear make way for the little rascal. It probably figured there was no glory in doing battle with it. In retrospect, I have come to believe now that the wolverine likely viewed me as an intruder and possible competitor for the ground squirrels. I don't suppose she had any previous experience with humans or else she might have been much more cunning and possibly have gotten a few bites in.

GREEN HILLS AND SWEET STEAKS

1964

ARE YOU ONE OF THOSE UNLUCKY nimrods who always has to battle for a place and the necessary time for a good enjoyable hunt? Do you have to fight your boss for time off – the second round with your pocketbook –- and the third round with the woman of the house until she throws in the towel to let you escape?

Perhaps you are more like Willie. He is another partner of a friend of mine and loves to hunt. A few years ago Willie and Billy, (I'll just call them by those names to protect the guilty) planned to hunt for moose. At the very last moment Willie's wife had other ideas and told him:

"Willie," she admonished, "if you go hunting again and drag another stinking beast into this house, I'll leave and find myself a real gentleman."

Willy appeared stunned for a moment and slowly with a sly smile he turned to her, kissed her on the cheek and said:

"You do that honey. I wish you a lot of luck."

The boys went hunting, shot two moose, but only Billy returned. Willie stayed hunting for three years. When he finally returned she still hadn't found herself a gentleman. Willie said, "This is because there ain't no such critter in this here town."

Here I must disagree with him for selfish reasons. However I've heard this sort of fight can break out in the best of families. On an average though, I guess the women folk are lucky that there aren't too many Willie's about.

But, when you stop to think for a moment, why did she get mad in the first place? Perhaps you'll find your own answer in this happy tale of where, how and when you can find new places to hunt while discovering a new concept of hunting.

For the past two dozen hunting seasons I've trampled over hill and dale from the Chilcotin mountains, to the Rockies, and north to the Atlin Lake area. I have pursued just about every existing legal game animal in this fantastic province of British Columbia. I wasn't too lucky in the beginning, but now I've worked out a pattern that not only keeps the freezer filled, it also helps my digestive system, and keeps mama at home and cooking.

Willie's problems were elementary. He's only one of many thousands of hunters who feel the urge to bring the bacon home, just like his forefathers did for thousands of years. He isn't like some modern man who kills just for the trophy. He spared no expense to bring home the meat – but it was for naught just the same.

Suppose one of your lucky friends — and this has happened to me — has shot that once-in-a-lifetime buck – but – generous fellow that he is – insists you accept a chunk of evil looking and even worse smelling venison for your Sunday dinner. Would you tell him to throw it away? Or would you simply accept it with many thanks and when no one is looking, quietly slip it into the garbage pail?

"What the hell died around here?" Was one of my friend's first questions when he came home for supper the other night after his wife had slaved over just such a nasty gift.

"Nothing," she replied. "It's that fancy moose roast you brought home." Well, that roast disappeared, and I'm sure you know where, but it could've been saved if the generous donor had known his game and when to shoot it and how to clean it.

More than half of a large mule deer buck occupies space in another friend's freezer. He killed it in 1960 during the very last weekend of the season. He hastily threw it away like the sack of neatly wrapped packages of deer I've found in the local dump.

You see it was the first really big trophy sized buck he'd ever seen, so he just had to shoot him. His wife has tried dozens of recipes, gallons of buttermilk and vinegar, and last but not least, heartbreaking prayers and believe me she's good at those. But every effort to make the meat edible resulted in miserable failure. The last time I inquired, she was desperately hunting for some exotic recipes. It seems she's heard something or other about Chinese cooks.

To find and shoot the game can be a costly and trying undertaking – but to cook and eat it can be the most repulsive experience of a lifetime.

Frank Kasa is a good friend and hunting partner of mine. He is also a connoisseur of the finer things in life. Frank loves good food... and a thick juicy venison steak which can 'make friends and influence people' for you, he said once.

"Look," he continued, "when you go to a butcher shop you'll have to pay a variety of prices for so-called Grade A meats. There is lean, fatty, and grain fed meat, and the current grass fed meat. But people are fussy and if you ever hand them the wrong roast, they'll get mighty suspicious of everything else you might offer them in the future."

Hunters should be some form of investment. It seems unreasonable that the game department spends public cash so that we can harvest the fruits of all their efforts – if all we ever do is to go out and blast some poor old bull moose – then leave him in the bush – or drop him off at the dump.

Two sportsmen I know shot two large bull moose in the Horsefly Lake area of BC. It was 8:30 in the morning. They had stalked the bulls and some cows for half an hour and had a ringside seat to the battle over the harem. After 15 minutes, when both animals were nearly exhausted and the younger bull was ready to leave, they shot and killed both. The boys came home and told many a tale of the fight, but little did they know what the excitement and the fighting did to the muscles and flavor of the meat of those bulls. They learned this much later after they paid the expensive butcher and locker bill.

I like to hunt before the mating season spoils the flavor of the meat. In British Columbia it is usually safe to shoot deer until the beginning of November. A lot depends of course on the weather and temperature. There is never a fast rule about certain areas and species. Elk can begin in the middle of August and I've heard the telltale bugling in the middle of October.

The moose of the Chilcotin start around the end of September and the mating season lasts; judging from my own observations; until the middle of November. Consequently I'm sure if he wants to fill his freezer with goodies a hunter must arrange his hunt for the proper time.

The hunting season in British Columbia usually runs from 1 September through to the last weekend in November with a few exceptions for certain Game Management Areas. The bulk of the game harvest, however doesn't come in until the snow flies and the meat of most animals is at its worst.

Many hunters don't believe in early hunting. They use the excuse of not having any "tracking snow" as the standard alibi. But I have often wondered how many times they have abandoned a perfectly fresh game track. This of course I can only answer for myself and must say, a good many times. It has often seemed unreasonable to follow a trail all day over the hills (they usually do point up hill, don't they?) to snow laden thickets and never do catch up with its maker. Or suddenly after a half day's tracking they lose faith in their own ability to determine the age of those tempting signs.

My new kind of hunting is just as successful as other methods and a great deal more enjoyable. I'd rather hunt in 50 above than in subzero temperatures, although this cannot always be avoided as you'll likely already know.

If you'd like to hunt elk in the East Kootenays of BC and bring good meat home… you must be prepared to put up with blizzards at the very end of the season. Only then has the elk had time to lose its rutting flavor. Then it once again becomes fit for a king's table.

The hunter won't even have to climb high mountains, and he misses much of the excitement of watching and hearing the big bulls bugle in the high meadows. He'll never see the splendor of the autumn forest, but he can eat his steaks when he gets them.

By comparison, the hunter of the Alpine pastures works a little harder for his game… but has certain compensations for his troubles… like the absence of large hunting crowds.

Last fall, Frank Kasa and I hunted McGillivray Pass and Eldorado Mountain. We were actually on our way home and had just stopped to look into a little side canyon. I climbed a tree for a good look around when suddenly I saw a large 'muley' buck perhaps 500 yards away and feeding at the base of a cliff. While I was watching he rubbed his huge antlers on some willow bush to tear off the dried velvet which looked like prize ribbons on a steer.

Frank agreed to wait for me while I climbed and waded through waist-high flowers and willows into shooting range. I had perhaps covered 100 yards when I noticed warm moose signs and regular trails which cut through the soft soggy canyon floor. The buck was out of my sites from here and by the time I reached a better place, a lonely clouded drifted in and hid the buck within its white misty folds. I was forced to wait.

I figured I had a chance to get my name into the record book. Instead I was sitting on pins and needles. 10 minutes can't really last that long but it seemed longer than the odds in the Irish Sweepstake. When the cloud was gone so was the buck.

I searched for him of course, but minutes later as I walked around a mound of rocks, the black hulk of the moose popped out of the flowers and trotted straight up the canyon side. With the crash of my shot he fell backwards into the ever present flowers. He was large for the area. His large antlers with five points on either side were still partly covered with soft velvet.

Why had he been in this canyon? We circled the area and followed some of his tracks and trails to find out where he'd come from. I followed what seemed to be the main route through some very dense willows and suddenly found myself in a beautiful little pasture about 50 yards x 50 yards square. At a glance it looked like 100 moose had bedded here. Every few steps the grass had been trampled to the ground. It must've been paradise for the bull ... for all the signs appeared to be made by him alone.

This is the moose way of life during the summer and when he has a choice he gets almost too fat to run. By the time mating season is over he has become as lean and sour is a dirty old dishrag. Nature in its strange and sometimes unexplainable ways mistreats the male members of the moose and deer family. The buck and bulls have to face hardships of winter in a comparatively poor physical condition – especially the deer.

If you need another good reason for an early hunt just imagine the gorgeous colors of the dying summers. They'll entice you to expose miles of film.

One can never tell what he'll run into on an early hunt and should be well prepared. For a gun, any scope-sighted rifle from the 7 mm up will do. But remember you might have to kill a grizzly as well.

Take the gun you trust and shoots the best. Binoculars are a must and will save you many a step. Your bedroll should be light but warm since the night temperatures can drop below freezing. I found a lightweight plastic sheet ideal for a lean-to in case of rain or minor snowfall. Usually it's safe enough to hunt the plateaus until the end of September.

If you never waded through the brilliant oceans of flowers and meadow grass; and have never seen herds of trophy bucks browsing undisturbed by your presence; then my friends you ought to give it a try someday. Bring your camera.

My moose weighed in at 674 pounds and cost me $75 in those days for butchering, including the freezing and locker room for a year. Traveling expenses of $20 (1964 prices) per man don't really count since I would probably spend more money on other possible hobbies. If I may respectfully request you to figure out the cash value of the moose you'll see, I'm sure it was a heck of a bargain.

P. S. Willie hasn't learned his lesson yet. But I saw his dear ex-wife in town the other day along with her new "gentleman" husband.

HUNTING THE ROCKY MOUNTAIN GOAT

October 1984

STANDING SENTRY, as if pasted against the background of dark rock on some of our tallest mountains, the Rocky Mountain Goat is probably our easiest-to-find big game animal. Although it can be found in our neighboring province, Alberta, some of the US Cascades states and Alaskan coastal regions – it is distinctly a British Columbia game species.

The trained eye can usually spot a goat from a considerable distance and has led many a hunter to stray into the realm of our most difficult and dangerous to hunt mountain goat on the North American continent. Indeed, to hunt the white goat (Oreamnus montanus) has become fashionable over the past three decades. It wasn't always this way – leastwise not in the early 1950s when I was first introduced to these creamy-white, shaggy, and short horned critters. Since then I have searched my soul to learn just what it is that makes a hunter climb to dizzying heights, onto dangerous cliffs, and over moving rockslides in pursuit of this generally phlegmatic animal.

Having hunted goats many times with varying degrees of success, I tend to believe that famous and illustrious writers, such as the late Jack O'Connor and Grancel Fitz, of **Outdoor Life Magazine** fame, (the latter known also as the organizer of the ***Boone and Crockett Club Game Trophy Records***) had a lot to do with this increasing goat hunting.

It seems only a handful of hardy, adventurous souls hunted goats back in the 50's. From my own experience, I recall that goat hunters were often regarded with the same courtesy one affords the village idiot. They were poor devils indeed, who... "simply didn't have enough brains to stay on safe and level ground."

In fairness to Grancel Fitz, I should relate here that he had already considered the mountain goat to be our most dangerous game. What he meant was, that a goat had only to be present on the dangerous-to-climb mountain to cause the unwary hunter considerable harm. After all, that poor devil only had to slip once… with little forethought and he could ascend to the pearly gates or slip and tumble down into hell without being stopped by anyone on the way.

In this, and most other assessments of goat hunting, the good Mr. Fitz was quite well-informed. I learned to appreciate his wisdom rather quickly although my first goat hunt was not a spectacular occasion.

I saw my first goat from the safety of level ground. The big 'Billy'; as it was; was about 400 meters above me among some trees that grew out of the road and crumbling cliffs. At first I had no intention of climbing up there… and I didn't want to shoot him… but my good partner egged me on.

"What are you waiting for? You've got a good, accurate rifle with a scope yet – you'll never get another chance like this!"

He never knew just how true his prediction really was. From the solid rest position I fired a single shot that was aimed about a foot over the 'Billy's' shoulder hump. He simply dropped and that was it. At the time I was using my first real big game rifle… a custom-made Mauser 30-06 caliber using a 180 grain Dominion soft-nosed bullet. My partner was jubilant.

"You got him!" He had watched through his field glasses and because of the fading light said, "Tomorrow morning, at first light – we'll go get him, eh?"

Indeed we recovered him, but it wasn't without hard work. He was a large 'Billy' weighing at least 150 kg. The 'Billy' hadn't fallen in the normal way either. His bearded chin had become stuck in the fork of a tree branch. He had only dropped to his knees but stayed upright all night. Skinning him I found that my bullet had pierced his heart and killed him instantly. His horns measured (in 1955 terms) 8.2 inches and had thick bases.

When he was later measured according to the prescribed standards of the Boone and Crockett club, someone told me he should be in the book with his combined   5/8 and three-quarter points. My partner mailed these measurements to New York, but I never learned whether my 'Billy' ever got into the trophy book.

I never thought too highly of trophy hunting for prestige reasons. My partner, bless his soul, commented that all one really needs is an accurate-shooting rifle… and know how to shoot at long-range and "Bingo, you've got yourself a goat!"

Yes, you bet. I was tempted to believe him, because I wanted to believe, and because I was still awfully green as far as hunting was concerned. But the day came soon enough for me when I cursed mountain goats, and all the mountains on which they live. My partner though, optimist that he was, didn't live long enough to see this transformation in me. Goats didn't do him in – he and another buddy both drowned when their canoe overturned while duck hunting on the Fraser River in December 1956. I still miss them both.

One other hunt remains vivid in my memory. It happened in the East Kootenays, in the watershed of the Palliser River. I was with a different partner. At the end of the logging road we stopped for lunch and spotted this white dot on the lower cliffs of the steep rock face. That did it. It drew us like a magnet.

It was a single goat that stood placidly on the cliff and looked down on us. After a brief consultation we decided that I, having a telescopic sight should try to shoot it. Besides, the rocks didn't look too difficult to climb, if that should become necessary – or so we figured.

"Don't worry," my partner said, "if you kill him he'll fall right down into the creek and we can fish him out from there."

"Killing it should be easy," I replied remembering my previous success. "It's only a 200 yard shot at the most. He'll never know what hit him."

Resting the rifle over a large boulder, I aimed carefully, and squeezed a shot off as perfectly as I could.

The goat staggered under the bullet impact, made his last wobbly steps forward and fell. But not off his perch. No, right at the edge of the cliff he dropped dead.

"Well, we shall have to climb up and get him, eh?"

My partner nodded.

There was a wide crack in the rock face angling up toward the goat and I decided to make good use of it. In the beginning the going was fine, easy, and safe enough. But as we gained altitude – that crack became much narrower, until finally it provided only the smallest of finger and toe holds.

My partner called for a halt. He was suddenly just as white as a goat and as petrified as the rock itself. It seemed he had made the mistake of looking down and became paralyzed with fear. He could no longer move. I too, became frightened. I didn't relish the thought of losing him straight down the rock face.

Only after a long spell, during which I talked soothingly to him, did I manage to get him down again and one healthy piece. But this climb had left its effects on me as well. Together we searched for another route to climb. There was none. Finally, after much cussing, I accepted my duty to retrieve the goat. I left my rifle behind and tried that same climb again. This time alone.

Within just a few feet of the goat I ran out of finger holds. There was only smooth rock left to conquer. Within a long arms reach lay the dead 'Billy'. Yet he may as well have been on the moon. From here I saw that he lay on some sharp rock points which prevented him from falling off his cliff. I saw his horns – massive, long, black and shiny. I guessed them to be at least a foot long. This Billy was a candidate for the world record if I ever saw one.

I shed a tear for him, as he lay there out of reach. Yet, I realized there was no humanly way possible that he could be salvaged. In the end, I was only too happy to get back off that treacherous mountainside and still have my own skin intact. I also learned that ascent is not necessarily the hardest part of mountain climbing.

On my earlier goat hunts I made a number of elementary mistakes. Once I tried to take a shortcut coming off the mountain. It was a route I hadn't previously seen. This was a serious mistake. Many times on that unforgettable descent I found myself on dead end rock shelves and had to climb up again to find detours. This was a nerve-racking experience I will not try to repeat again.

Another time I came down a steep slope. It consisted mainly of fine rubble and I thought at first this would be the way to go. Suddenly a large chunk of rugged real estate came loose behind me. Just in the nick of time I had the presence of mind to run sideways. The loose stuff carried me down a few meters, but I got out of the way of a huge rock slide. It thundered past me and left me speechless for a while. It had been a trap of my own making of course.

Remembering those early mistakes, I believe now that any serious goat hunter ought to take some serious lessons in mountaineering before he is turned loose to hunt mountain goats or sheep. Such foresight will not necessarily be easier on the game, but it will definitely be easier on the hunter's family.

One particularly good friend and hunting partner comes to mind whenever I think of mountain goats, and I don't suppose that fact will ever change for me. We used to hunt in truly rough terrain without incident or trouble. He was tough. He thought nothing of climbing the highest mountains… always causing me problems trying to keep up with him. One fateful day, however he was hunting goats again with a different partner in an area that I had never liked, because of its extreme ruggedness.

A large search party found them a few days later at the bottom of a cliff. They had slipped on the moss cover of a wet rock face and their time ran out.

A few years after this terrible accident, I was tempted to hunt some goats on the eastern face of Cathedral Mountain, where it rises steeply out of the glacier blue waters of Atlin Lake. I figured it wouldn't be particularly difficult to get within shooting range. When it began to rain, suddenly, without warning, the rocks became as slippery as a bathtub full of soap and bath oil.

Yes, you had better believe I thought an awful lot about my dear, dead friend on that day. I could feel rigor mortis setting in long before I reached the bottom of that hillside again. Furthermore, I solemnly promised all the goats on that mountain, that I would never, ever disturb them again! Believe me, I kept my promise!

These days my hunting is pretty much restricted to areas that are absolutely safe to climb, such as the time when Horst Pothmann and I hunted goats from my canoe. Actually we hunted moose, but it came to pass that I saw band of goats in a large willow patch on the shoulder of a mountain at Llewellyn Inlet on Atlin Lake.

These were the days before special restrictions came into force for that area. But again it rained. The bush was soaking wet and within a very short time water was splashing around inside our hip-waders. Wearing hip-waders on a moose hunt is often a brilliant idea – alas, not so for hunting goats. The trouble was... we had no other footwear handy.

The goats somehow managed to spot us and likely had previous experiences with other hunters. They headed straight for the horizon. Two of them made it safely, but the last one in the bunch fell to Horst's 30-06. This was his first goat and was totally unplanned for this trip in our area. After this he felt goat hunting was rather easy. All wouldn't have worked out well though had we not found a serviceable cabin to dry out in overnight, before we returned to Atlin, some 50 miles away. The goat had to make the trip lashed to the outrigger of the canoe and it easily became the whitest goat I have ever seen.

For all my many seasons of goat hunting I have but one trophy to show. Of course, many times I got quite close to goats. I have studied them, photographed them, and been with partners who were successful. I just don't care to kill another one. After my first, fluky success, I have learned that goats are nobody's patsy. I have watched some hunters uncork hands-full of shells just to bring down a single goat. I have learned that they can carry an awful lot of lead if not hit in a vital area.

Goats are smart enough to avoid danger — especially if they have been hunted before. They will not stick around like a target on the rifle range. Therefore, the goats at Atlin Lake were always quick to head for the highest summits as soon as they heard a motor on the lake. I watched two hunters try their luck with them and even before they reached their boat – the goats had hoofed it up over the top of the mountain. They knew exactly what was coming and certainly knew how to avoid it.

Some figures published by the B.C. Fish and Wildlife Branch claimed we have about 100,000 goats in the province, and only about 2000 - 3000 are harvested annually. I am inclined to believe this, because I have seen large bands of goats and the hunter-success ratio being what it is – our total global population isn't in danger of being over-exploited. Most goats are totally inaccessible by legal means. It is only in areas close to human access where goats become vulnerable. Even then, I would much rather bet on a goat's survival than on the hunter's success.

By and large B.C. Hunter's hunt for meat and that is basically as it should be. A trophy goat that is tough and stringy like a prize-fighter is not really considered a delicacy. I have eaten goat meat on several occasions and have found a young mountain goat tasty and edible, indeed.

Since a mountain goat is not related to the goats of the domestic variety, but rather belongs to the antelope family, a young animal is to some of my acquaintances a delicacy. But most goat hunters are looking for trophy-sized animals with the beautiful white, woolly hide, and large dagger-like horns.

Many reason that it is much easier to kill a moose or deer for meat. It is not an easy job to carry a goat off a mountain. It will be very interesting to see how the new anti-waste laws affect goat hunting. Of course, one can expect that someone will soon find loopholes in that bit of well intended legislation.

Among the many tasks a goat hunter faces, the most difficult, perhaps, is that of identifying a trophy-sized goat when only that one goat can be seen and not compared to another. I have seen hunters kill young kids in the terribly mistaken belief that it was an adult animal. When family units of goats can be seen, it isn't too difficult to determine which ones are the adults.

Usually there are 'Billy's in any large band of goats. Trophy animals though, like to spend their days alone, or in the company of another male. In any case the hunter is well advised to use high magnification glassware to determine if a specific animal is worth his sweat, effort and risk. The size of gleaming, black horns are hard to estimate at a long distance.

Although both sexes grow horns, the male goat's horns are usually thicker in diameter and evenly curved, while the female's horns are quite slender and usually show a distinct little hook at the tips. To be in the trophy class, the horns should measure about 1 foot or, to help with the guessing – about one fourth the total height of the animal – without counting the shoulder hump. One fellow I know once thought the horn should be about the length of the goat's face. He killed his goat only to find that the animal was a perfect small-scale model of a big 'Billy'.

Goat horns display similar growth rings such as the horns of mountain sheep, but they are much less pronounced and practically invisible at a distance. It simply takes much experience, hard work, and good educated guessing to bag a trophy goat. Accurate long-range shooting might eventually kill a goat, but it may still be a great disappointment when you see it up close.

To estimate shooting distances in goat habitat is also quite tricky. Some hunters feel it is good enough to rough guess, fire one shot, to see where the bullet strikes the rocks, and adjust their aim accordingly. This is a good way to cripple animals – that is about all. In the far northern regions of our provincial range estimating distance and size can be unbelievably tricky.

One of my partners once saw what he thought to be a big 'Billy' on the North Slope of Mount Ewing, near Atlin, B. C. He decided it was worth the effort and scrambled like mad to hunt that animal. At nightfall he returned to our camp depressed.

He confessed his erstwhile estimate had been wrong. "Sure enough it was a 'Billy', that the little fellow had only about 6 inch horns. I let him go."

A week later, while hunting on the same mountain for caribou we learn something about range estimation. We saw a band of 13 caribou, including two large bulls, at what we estimated was no more than 300 m. Since our rifles were sighted in at that that distance, we thought we had our game in the bag. Well, 13 shots later, the caribou disappeared over the horizon unhurt.

Dumbfounded we began to pace off the range. 700 odd steps later we stopped counting. It was quite obvious that all our shooting had done no harm. We pondered for some time about how the super-pure atmosphere of that northern country could fool experienced marksmen from the south. But it happens all the time.

One morning on that same mountain, I saw what I took to be a grizzly on the hillside above us. My partner thought so too, and tugged on my sleeve.

"Hold it! We don't want to be hunting grizzlies!"

"He is a long way off," I replied thinking of our previous experiences. "Let's get a little closer so we can have a good look at him, eh?"

We hiked another 50 paces and had the laugh of our lives. The presumed grizzly suddenly became just a marmot standing sentry over his burrow no more than 100 meters away. This, I must confess was nearly the worst range estimation I ever made.

About 35 years ago I hunted goats near Bralorne with George Hoy, late of Richmond, B. C. We experienced a rough go, mostly climbing over crumbling cliffs to about 9000 feet (2700 m). We'd seen the goats from below and thought it was possible to get one or two. We took overnight equipment along so we could spend the night on the mountain if it became necessary.

Well, it was necessary, and proved to be a very wise precaution. It was nearly supper time before we even reached the summit of that mountain. George set out to hunt right away, while I set up our camp so we wouldn't have to fumble around in the dark later on.

A storm blew in with alternating rain, snow, and hail showers. Suddenly lightning flashed all about us. Of course, our goats had disappeared somewhere. Nevertheless, George continued to pursue them along a precarious ridge trail from where he could see both sides of the mountain below. I was too tired from the strenuous climb and stayed in camp cook for us. I still shudder though, when I recall seeing George on the highest point of land for some miles around amid all that thunder and lightning. Of course he survived that experience… but found no goats. Just before dark he returned to camp and a good night sleep.

At first light the sound of rolling stones awoke us. Peeking out from under our shelter we saw the same band of six goats on the ridge trail no more than 200 m away. By the time we had dressed, a cloud rolled in and hid them from view.

"That's just great!" George lamented. "Well, at least they won't be able to spot us either, eh?"

We scrambled up the ridge after them. We could hear them all the time, but in that soggy, milky cloud – we just couldn't see them. We spent all morning hunting and by noon we had to leave for the drive home. Halfway down the mountain we looked back one more time and saw the cloud was gone. The goats? Oh yes, they were still there, resting and chewing their cud. I had the feeling that they were probably laughing at us.

Judging from these and many other first-hand experiences, I too, must conclude that mountain goats are indeed the toughest of all the North American big game to hunt – if not the most dangerous. Surely there are occasions when one can be taken without a great deal of effort, but in general terms I think they are as hard to kill as a grizzly bear, and they can carry just as much lead before the drop. If they are not killed instantly, one usually loses them to the terrain.

Any of the medium-sized big game cartridges will do a good job on goats if used appropriately. Then again, I have seen goats disappear over the ridges with more than one bullet in them. The greatest mistake a hunter can make is to shoot at extreme distances. Few bullets are designed to maintain their mushrooming qualities at long ranges.

Without that shocking power some of these bullets will shoot right through the animal without causing the massive tissue and bone destruction necessary to bring the animal down. Personally I prefer rifles in the 7 mm to 30-06 caliber class because I have this secret phobia of being kicked right off the mountain by the brutal recoil of larger calibers.

Finally, I must re-emphasize that serious hunters should learn at least the fundamentals of mountaineering techniques, and be appropriately outfitted, before attempting to chase mountain goats around. Like I said earlier – it may only be a hard climb up – but coming down again – in one healthy piece – is quite another matter. Remember too, once you have killed your goat – you will have to go get it back to camp. At least as much of it as the law and common decency prescribes.

"WILD ANIMALS — WHAT WILL THEY DO NEXT?"

THE PRIVATE LIVES OF WILD animals are often quite puzzling to humans who are basically too close to the old grindstone to see over or around it. To be sure they often do things which, from our point of view, are hard to fathom. They may appear peculiar at times, or hilariously funny, all are – I am certain – quite dramatic.

So, I suppose, I shall never learn or understand what possessed a California Bighorn ram to step into the way and block the path of my saddle horse one evening, right after a hard day's hunt for sheep in British Columbia's Ashnola country. It was near Juniper Creek where a horse trail had been cut through thick pine growth by a long-time friend of mine, who held a guiding license for big game in that territory. It was near sunset. My old saddle mare gingerly picked her way through the stumps. Suddenly she was surprised by a young ram that just popped out of the brush and refused to budge. I can still hear his "bahhhhhh" as he looked at me.

My horse stopped, and since the ram wouldn't move either, it came to pass that I began a rather one-sided conversation with him.

"What are you trying to do, huh? Collect a toll fee maybe? Does your mother know you're out here making a nuisance of yourself?"

"Bahhh", came his answer. He was honey blond in color, and his sickle horns betrayed his tender age.

Of course, he was fully protected at the time with his 3/4 horn-curl minimum size regulation, and it was easy to tell that his slender horns were less than half-curl in length.

"What am I going to do with you, huh?"

Again, he "bahhhed" in reply. I urged my horse forward, thinking that the ram would step aside at least.

But the old horse wouldn't push this juvenile off the trail. Finally, I dismounted and lead the horse ahead.

The ram stepped aside, but only far enough to let us past at arm's length. I could have touched him.

When I remounted and rode on towards camp, he followed us bleating as if he had just lost his mother. Within sight of our camp, he eventually stopped, uttered a final "Bahhh", and headed back up to the mountain. Later, it dawned on me I should have checked further to see what he needed... Perhaps he was trying to get me to help out another sheep in distress.

On this and many other hunts in the same area, I often saw flocks of sheep, usually ewes and lambs who allowed a very close approach. In fact, one morning I managed to obtain a snapshot of a sheep, a mule deer, and a Hereford cow – all in one picture.

Of course, no one should conclude from this story that sheep hunting is easy, because the legal-sized patriarchs of the species do behave quite differently. They are usually so shy that a hunter must have the luck of the Irish to first win a limited entry license. He must be even luckier to get within effective rifle range of a trophy-sized ram.

That night in camp, I asked my guiding friend about such contrasting behaviour.

"Well," he drawled, "they ain't stupid, if that's what you mean. The ones that get shot – they are the stupid ones – they have made a fatal mistake. If it weren't for their occasional mistakes – you and I, my boy – we'd be out of business."

I must have looked sceptical so he continued:

"Look at it this way – we are in their living room here – we can't hear half as good as they can – are comparatively blind – and our noses – hell, I can't smell you after you've been unwashed for a week. No sir, every time one of them big rams gets himself killed – it's their bloody mistake. You can take my word for it."

Mind you, not too many eager hunters want to agree with me on that score. They think that they are smarter'n the sheep. They like to brag about it too. Hey, don't get me wrong, there's nothing wrong with tellin' a good story, is there?"

"Reckon not. Otherwise, it would be a pretty dull world, huh?"

"Right you are, my boy, but I have met some guys that act like some smart-ass undertakers who think they are clever when accidents or natural catastrophe gives their business an unexpected special boost. Think about that some, huh. We all make mistakes daily. Just usually not fatal ones."

The incident with the ram was not an isolated case, because on another occasion a mule deer doe and her fawn walked right up to me while I sat on a stump and smoked my pipe. They had approached down-wind, only God knows why, and they stopped only when I reached out to touch and pet them. Then, of course, they bolted away in their familiar great leaps and bounds.

Of all the animals I have ever hunted, the timber wolf is probably the most clever and least likely to make mistakes.

When called, I have seen foxes and coyotes come right up without great hesitation. Sometimes they are over-confident, thinking they can fool this old hunter all the way.

Timber wolves however, have come into my camps, but always made absolutely sure they wouldn't be seen.

I recall one year's hunt near Atlin, B.C., when three large hunting parties had nine moose carcasses dressed and quartered, hanging all about the campsite.

The wolves came every night and howled as if they were at the Salvation Army singing for a decent supper. They did, of course, get our scraps. But one night I could actually hear a wolf sniffing at the tent canvas. Nevertheless, we never got to see hide nor hair of a wolf that night.

On another occasion we spotted some eagles flying over what we thought might be a carcass. Bruno and I walked over to the carcass. We found it was only three hundred steps. When we arrived, the eagles departed. They just soared above to see what we would leave them.

The carcass was that of a large bull moose, and aside from one missing haunch, was almost intact. We found the bull had been shot by a trophy hunter who had only hack-sawed the skull plate with the antlers off the head, and left the rest behind to rot.

A wolf was also present and with a steady lope he departed rather quickly. But upon inspection we saw he had operated as cleanly as a surgeon. The piece of meat he had taken away with apparent ease would have been a hefty load for a man. We circled the plateau because we figured the wolf might have a den nearby. Alas, we never found it.

While big game hunting, I found that it can be almost equally exciting to watch other, smaller animals. One particular red squirrel was absolutely hilarious.

It decided to investigate me while I held an afternoon siesta in my camper. Bold as brass, it came through the open door and poked its nose into every nook and cranny it found.

She ran right over top of me, but when I remained still, it carried on with its inspection of the premises. The only item that was easily accessible to the squirrel was a large coconut that lay on the table. As soon as she saw the nut, her behaviour changed. I could swear her face lit up like that of a gold prospector who suddenly stumbled into his Eldorado.

I could see the little rascal smile as she put her tiny paws on the nut.

"That's mine now," she seemed to say. "All mine!"

But then her problems started. First, she tried to lift the nut. No go. The nut was probably much heavier than the squirrel. She tried to chew on it but couldn't get her teeth into it. Finally she discovered the nut would roll.

Thump! She had it on the floor. In very short order she had the nut outside on the ground yet still there was no way for her to open it.

Her smile had now vanished. She sat by that nut and chattered like a machine gun calling for help.

I stepped outside and split the nut with the camp axe. I hadn't yet re-sunk the axe into the chopping block when she had grabbed one-half of the shell and climbed the nearest tree with it. She got as far as the first branch.

Try as she might to keep moving it was to no avail. Her shell got hung up. The poor thing worked herself into a sweat trying to sneak the nut past that branch. Finally, she lost her grip and her coconut chunk fell down. Instead of eating her prize right there – all afternoon she tried the same stunt over again.

Each time the nut fell, she would hunker down beside it and berate the "damn" thing in a very noisy way. Finally, towards evening, she took both halves into some bushes and I never saw her again.

In a far northern hunting camp once, close to a lake full of fighting pike, I experienced my fish catch disappearing, but I couldn't figure out how.

On the beach, close to my camp, lay an old wreck of a plywood boat. It was useless except for its decks which provided a great table for filleting and cleaning fish.

Since the pike fishing was excellent with individual catches of between eight and fifteen pounds, I had prepared a lot of fish for smoking. Some I had just cleaned, scaled, and washed, while others were filleted for camp consumption.

I kept the fish on the slanting decks for draining. Since the weather was cool, I had no worries about spoilage. After covering the fish with a clean, damp burlap sack, I had no concerns about leaving them outside overnight.

In the morning, the largest fish was missing. There were no other campers in the area and the thief had left no tell-tale tracks. After a little consideration, I figured that maybe an eagle or osprey had taken the fish. I wasn't too concerned with the loss, because it was easily replaced, but my curiosity was certainly aroused.

I kept a close watch. The next morning, another fish was missing. The burlap had remained almost totally in place. For nearly a whole week this thieving continued, until one morning, when I got up earlier than usual. I saw one of my pike slither through the tall grass around the boat's bow, and determined to get into a hole under it.

Just in the nick of time, I grabbed the fish tail and hung on. It wasn't easy! Finally, using my handkerchief to provide a better grip on the slippery pike, I pulled it free of the boat.

I was not prepared for what followed. An almost pure white mink appeared from the hole. It was in a fighting mood. With flashing, chattering teeth, it made a grab for the fish and latched onto its head.

Surprised, I let go, and in less time than it takes to tell about it – my fish was gone for good.

With a bit of snare wire, I booby-trapped every suspicious hole around the boat. Nothing much happened. But, the following morning, another fish was missing.

I never caught the mink, but what puzzled me most was… what would a tiny mink whose weight is measured in ounces, really, do with all that fish?

In total, the cagy mink stole 50 to 60 pounds of fish from me during that single week.

Since the boat wreck was too large and heavy for me to move, I never did find out more.

Unlike a mink in the grass, some animals leave more peculiar trails that may be just as difficult to unravel.

A logging-contractor friend of mine found this out.

"One of my fallers had left a whole case of chainsaw oil in the bush for the winter," he told me."

"He figured it would be quite safe from theft or vandals because the area we were in was quite mountainous and steep. It would be covered by about twenty feet of snow during winter.

Well, following spring he comes back to his cache and finds every single can punctured and empty. All cans showed four holes. For a while we thought that some clown had come in after all and used the cans for plinking practice.

When he told me about it we posted a whole lot of signs around our operations."

NO TRESPASSING! NO SHOOTING!

"You, you know the kind, huh?"I nodded.

"Then, one fine day here comes a fellow with a rifle, said he hadn't seen the signs. I gave him hell. I told him what had happened to our oil and showed him some o' those empty cans."

"Says this smart fellow: 'No bullets ever made holes like that. Bullets go in and out. These holes all go inward only. They look like tooth marks to me."

"We pondered that for a while. I mean who-in-hell will chew oil cans an' drink the stuff, huh? "

A few days later my faller comes back to camp to get more oil.

"What's the damn matter with your saw?" I asked. "Got an oil leak?"

'No,' he grins, 'it's not the saw, but now I know who done it. It's a bloody grizzly. Saw him an hour ago. He had a can of oil in his teeth, stood on his hind legs and guzzled the oil like you drink beer."

My friend laughed. "Honest, I have seen him too, now. That damn bear guzzles Quaker State Oil like you'n me drink Coke. That clown could make a commercial and get rich."

"Yeah, but wouldn't that stuff be harmful?" I asked.

"Dunno," he answered. "He is still around sometimes. Kinda harmless, too.

We just call him 'Slippery Joe' – after the trail he leaves sometimes.

SHEEP HUNTING ANYONE?

THE EXCITING IDEA OF HUNTING wild sheep preoccupies a considerable number of hunters annually. Some are indeed obsessed with these ideas and will do just about anything until they have actually experienced such a hunt.

    I know. I used to be like that once. There was a time when I was just as enthusiastic about sheep hunting as my dog is about a juicy steak – or a bitch in heat. Yes, sheep hunters are like that. Once they have seen the majestic sheep ranges, climbed about in the wind and shale – they want to go back for more.

Well, times have changed. Today's hunter must plan even better than ever before. In most instances he must be lucky enough to draw a special license for the specific area in which he or she is permitted to hunt for sheep. This relatively new system of "SHEEP MANAGEMENT" dictates well in advance where and how to hunt and so forth – therefore a number of important factors must be considered.

For instance: the luck of the draw practically limits where the hunter must hunt. It dictates whether he will fly into an open area, backpack – or whether he may be able to drive in and hike up. I have hunted sheep via three different methods, and must say that my hunts on horseback were always the most enjoyable. They offered me the greatest potential for success, and were the least strenuous for me. Fly-in and backpacking trips from a high lake base camp can be very tough experiences I found out. I don't recommend them for anyone who is not in top physical condition, or not very experienced in backpack camping.

This is not the lazy person's approach to sheep hunting. With horses, the rider can let his mount roam for considerable distances. But the foot-slogger who finds himself in a sheep area can only go so far without a horse. Should he be lucky and bag the allotted trophy – he will be required by law to pack the animal out as well.

Of course, that is why you must gather all the right information concerning access and just what is involved before you can become lucky. The right information might enable the hunter to drive into a good sheep range, like I did once, and intercept them as they cross from one range to another. I used a trail bike and also transported my Stone sheep the 20 odd kilometers back to my camp on it.

There are limitations to bike travel. If someone wishes to survive such a hunt without breaking their bones – I wouldn't attempt it like two hunters I once met in the Ashnola country and who were riding their bikes on horse or game trails. On opening morning of the season, I was after California Bighorn's and rode along Ewart Creek on my way to Juniper Creek in the high country. It is about 5 to 6 km from the end of the road to where Ewart Creek must be crossed on the log bridge. From there the trail leads straight towards heaven.

Great was my surprise when I suddenly came upon two bike riders who had experienced an accident. One of the men had broken his bike, and judging by his groans, some ribs as well. They didn't know the country very well. To me, who has hunted there a number of times, their attempt seemed to border on lunacy. I was glad the trail had stopped them, I must confess, because the last thing a sheep hunter needs – is some noisy bike running along the ridges.

All Bighorn Sheep like the high country. They can run better uphill than down. Albeit, the California sub-species, when disturbed, do seem to prefer to escape downhill into creek bottoms and thickets. I have witnessed this behavior on several occasions. But, because I wasn't prepared for their tactics, I missed several opportunities to bag rams. Not so, your average Rocky Mountain Bighorn, or Stone sheep. They will climb as high as they can get so quickly you will begin to wonder how it could be possible.

My own greatest obstacle to sheep hunting was the usual lack of good horses and pack animals to take me into sheep ranges which are not overrun by weekend hunters. To be frank, horses were sometimes available, but not at a price I could afford.

Yes, let's face it, sheep hunting has always been a rather expensive hobby, and you can bet your last raise – it is even more expensive today. My horseback hunts were made possible by my good friend, the well-known Princeton, B.C. outfitter and guide, Pat Wright who annually guided sheep hunters in the Ashnola watershed. Nevertheless, I hunted for seasons before I managed to bag my first ram.

The Ashnola country is indeed one of the finest hunting areas in British Columbia. It is about a 450 mile square area as the map shows it, but that does not include all the ups and downs. On one trip we packed a jack-camp into the high Cathedral Mountains, up to the Haystack and Ladyslipper lakes. I saw no sheep that time, but enjoyed some good fishing and excellent deer hunting.

The scenery there is so beautiful. Even on a non-productive trip is worth the effort and expense. One word of caution however – the hunter who plans to hike into those areas had better be as strong as a pack horse. If he shoots game – he must be as tough as two horses at least.

In B.C. we have two main species of Bighorn sheep: the Rocky Mountain and the California

Bighorns. The latter being a sub species… albeit native to this province. There are also the thin horn sheep – the Dall and Stone Sheep of the northern mountains. All can be confusing to the beginner.

The new manual for the B. C. Hunter Training Course, compiled under the auspice of the fish and wildlife branch, is not very specific about identifying all sheep. Among the Stone Sheep there are a number of color variations such as the black sheep or 'Ovis Dalli Niger', the Saddleback, or 'Ovis Dalli Fanini' and the Liard sheep, 'Ovis Dalli Liardensis'.

Judging by the government's new description of Stone Sheep, a hunter may easily believe all Stone Sheep are white, when in fact all shades of color from white to black may be found. Then again, the Stone Sheep of the Atlin, B. C. area are the smallest in body size and they may be almost pure white. But, most that I have seen were light gray or with bluish gray saddle marks.

Further south, near Muncho Lake, the sheep I have seen were dark brown, and the ewes and lambs there might be mistaken for Bighorns. Only the rare (in B.C.) Dall sheep are pure white. It is rather important that a hunter actually knows what to look for when searching for sheep in any given area.

On Marble Dome Mountain, just west of Gladys Lake, I once saw a young ram with half-curled horns at very close range and thought he was a Dall sheep. Back in 1968, it was still legal to kill a female sheep, and I recall my partner was awfully itchy to justify his effort and considerable hunting expenses. In the end I managed to persuade him not to kill that ram.

"If you take him now, he won't grow larger while wall mounted in your den, my friend. In time you will get tired of looking at that baby and likely cuss yourself for killing him. Let's come back next year, maybe you'll find real trophies and – or even in five years for this one, huh?" That did the trick.

When I first hunted California Bighorns in the Ashnola, the legal size for rams was three-quarter horn curl or larger. Anyone could hunt them. This particular herd contained about 75 legal sized rams I was informed by the Fish and Wildlife Branch staff. The average annual kill was about six rams. It wasn't easy, even on horseback, to get within shooting range of the trophy ram. (Just the other day it was in the paper that there were only 27 California Bighorn sheep left in that area December 1991 – so something has gone terribly wrong with their system.)

I recall one afternoon when I rested my horse near the trail to Joe Lake. It was on a rather rough hillside that was strewn with dead and upturned trees. Suddenly my horse pointed uphill and to my left. I looked up. There, on my left, at a breakneck pace were a bunch of rams pouring off the hill. The leader was a chocolate-brown ram with fully curled horns.

Oh boy, I'm going to be lucky this time, I thought. Crouching low I slid a cartridge into my rifle chamber.

There were six rams in single file angling towards me and ready to cross my trail 100 yards in front of me. The largest ram was in the lead but even the last one was still a legal size trophy.

"Keep a-coming," I prayed as I aimed at the leader's chest.

With my elbow resting on the log I found it easy to keep the crosshairs on his massive front quarter. At the last moment I swung the gun site to his brisket to allow for his speed and fired. In the scope I saw something white flying about, but the ram didn't falter as expected. He didn't even stumble as he crossed into some heavy timber.

Had I missed? I wasn't really sure and couldn't understand why the ram didn't fall. I had enough time to reload and shoot again at the straggler. I didn't. The rams disappeared. With my binoculars I looked at the spot where the ram had been when I fired.

Oh yes, there was something white. I left the horse and walked over to investigate. It was an upturned tree root that had obstructed my bullet. I found the wood chip that I had seen fly. There was no cut hair and no blood. I spent the whole day searching, downhill into the thickets and found nothing.

"Well, that's the way it is with sheep hunting," Pat Wright replied, when I related my experience to him. "A bullet is easily deflected when shooting at a moving target. A root gets in the way, and you don't even see it, because you're concentrating so hard."

When I bagged my ram the following year I had to thank the flock of magpies for it. I spent the whole afternoon glassing the hillsides where sheep might be… and somehow, after a hard day's ride, had dozed off to sleep. I wasn't used to riding regularly and had been up since 5 a.m. My legs and gluteus muscles ached and were quite sore.

When the sun had set behind the Cathedral's and the air became chilly, I awoke again. I put on my jacket, lit a smoke, and once more looked the hillside over very carefully. I noticed the birds fly across the canyon at my feet. They landed on some moving objects I had previously overlooked. Sheep!

There were three in all. But I was way too far away to make out any details. The evening air was still full of heat waves that rose from a rock slide – distorting their images.

"Here we go again," I whispered to the old horse. "There's no prize for some honest effort, huh?" I tightened the saddle cinches, mounted and rode down the canyon toward the sheep.

They were rams. The largest and darkest looking animal appeared to be legal size. I left the horse in a jack pine thicket and crawled on my belly to within shooting range. Finally, within 100 meters of the ram, and hidden behind a boulder, I made one last check with the binoculars. The ram was grazing. Being downhill of him, I couldn't determine with certainty that his horns were three-quarter curl.

The ram looked up and scratched his ear with the hind foot. When he resumed grazing I spent some time agonizing behind a boulder observing while trying to make up my mind about him.

The BC Hunting Regulation guide and its illustration of the legal sized ram printed in it made my decision. He was legal. He fell where he stood – surely not knowing what hit him. But I no longer enjoyed that hunt. I felt more like a bloody executioner.

Hunting ought to be spontaneous to be satisfying. More like it is in deer season, when the bucks are legal as long as they have grown a visible antler. Even from a stand, European-style, it is still quite exciting. But having to first start fishing around in my pocket for a picture – hell – that's no good. But this is how the new regulations prescribed sheep hunting. For a time the three-quarter curl regulation was abandoned. Suddenly it became legal to shoot, via the special license, ***any male sheep***.

I never returned there. Since then I have often wondered about a young ram who once followed my old horse around as if it was his mother. I wonder whether the young fellow had a chance to grow up and perpetuate himself, or if some lazy, ignorant shooter has his immature horns on the den wall?

When I questioned why this regulation came about the response was: "... to provide a quality hunting experience..." At least that was the excuse the Fish and Wildlife Branch guru's gave to my inquiries.

The Ashnola is no longer the remote area it used to be, although it is still a reasonably good choice for a hunter with a special sheep license. Other native ranges for the Californian's are the

Yalakom, The Camelsfoot, and Shulaps Ranges, north of Lillooet. They ranged north to the Taseko Lakes, the Gang Ranch Country, and Riske Creek.

To compare, Rocky Mountain Bighorn are very similar in appearance, but somewhat larger and chunkier than the Californian's. Their horns are more massive and curled tighter. The initiated can identify them just by looking at their ears. They are rounded and small, while the Californian's ears are somewhat pointed. The Californian ram average about 65k field dressed while the Rocky Mountain Bighorn ram will be weighing in the vicinity (live weight) of 150k.

Trophy hunters anxious to get their names into record books will be disappointed by the Californian's. The last time I looked there wasn't a single California Bighorn mentioned in the record books. Rocky Mountain Bighorn have been known to grow horns to a total length of 49.5 inches.

To compare again, if I recall correctly, the world record mountain sheep ram was a Stone Ram. It was killed by a chap near Chadwick near the headwaters of the Prophet River, in B. C., and had horns that measured some 51.5 inches along the outer curl of the horns. I would guess that a ram with horns of 44 inches and longer would indeed be a candidate for the book.

Over the years I have studied literally hundreds of sheep, close-up and through high-magnification glassware. I would estimate a Dall ram's live weight at perhaps, 90 k. which is about the same as the Atlin Stone Sheep would weigh. They cannot be mistaken for trophy sized mountain goats, although a bush pilot surprised me once when he told me the mountains around Surprise Lake, near Atlin, B.C. contained a lot of goats. Since I have hunted these mountains for 30 years and never saw goat there – ever — I have come to the conclusion that most of the white animals he saw were Stone Sheep.

I have done some flying in the Atlin area and found that in most regions it is the only economically reasonable way to get into sheep ranges. Nevertheless, that kind of hunting cannot compare to the old-fashioned horseback hunting. But it takes a special kind of person or nut who is willing to be dropped off in some of the last real wilderness this province has to offer, usually hundreds of miles from civilization, and should the need arise, from help.

Air travel isn't cheap either. In particular when the hunter wants to play it safe, and wishes to use adequate aircraft for the job. It has been my experience that a Cessna 185 on floats is probably the smallest aircraft a hunter should consider. Nevertheless, a party of two may find it just a little too tight and risky.

We tried to put two hindquarters of a caribou into such a plane once, and then take off from about at about the 4000 feet elevation mark. This was a no-go. We had to unload again and make two trips which certainly brought up the cost of transportation considerably. Nevertheless, we still wore some willow branches on the floats before we got back to civilization. This kind of flying is downright unhealthy. We should have made arrangements for a larger plane, such as a Beaver to pick us up.

Yes, flying in the northern wilderness can have its moments. Usually the novice hunter skimps on equipment and food so he can get by with the "cheaper aircraft". But then, he might also forget that weather is a major factor to be considered. You can easily spend $2000 on the trip, and find yourself sitting in a pup tent for a couple of weeks because of fog, rain, or snow. I even heard of hunting parties that were stranded for weeks. Their pilots hadn't forgot to pick them up again – the weather just wouldn't allow for it.

Another disadvantage is that the northern lakes are usually surrounded by swamps through which an aspiring sheep hunter must hop, skip and jump to gain a good shot of the mountains. In this location an innocent accident can have very serious consequences – especially if that aircraft isn't scheduled to return for a week or more. The obvious advantages however are, you are literally free as a bird and not likely crowded by other hunters.

Of course, with horses one isn't 100% safe either. You could get thrown and even break some bones. But two people hunting together can always help each other out. At least they can commiserate in a more comfortable camp.

The greatest issue with horses is that they need a lot of care. They must have adequate feed which is not always freely available during the latter part of the season in the rough terrain – plus they must be well shod. Tacking gear must be kept in good repair and – hunters must have a fair amount of horse-sense. Without that they are indeed asking for big trouble. The stereotype of a cowboy 'Meany' and that sort of stuff that brutalizes horses shouldn't even be in Hollywood movies never mind out on sheep trails.

Personally I find it most enjoyable when a sure-footed mountain horse does most of the really hard climbing for me. In that case I have the time to look for game… something I can't do while stumbling about on foot.

Sheep hunting is essentially 90% looking and spotting, systematically searching whole mountainsides with binoculars and spotting scopes. When they are finally found, their size is determined, and if of legal size, only then comes the actual foot stalking and the shoot.

Some folks find this sitting and glassing boring. I have hunted with partners who couldn't sit still for more than 10 minutes at a time. It is however, not unusual to spend the whole day in one likely observation post and do nothing but systematically glass the hillsides. Sheep do not always move about where you can spot them easily. Often they lie in an observation position watching me while chewing their cud.

There have been times when I was willing to swear that there was nothing alive among all the rocks and boulders only to be surprised when suddenly a band of rams pops up from a clump of Juniper and heads for Alberta. Those sheep have probably spotted the hunter the first moment he hiked over the ridge into their basin. They lie still, safely out of range, and entertain themselves for hours watching a busy hunter.

If the hunter did likewise – the possibility exists that the sheep will eventually forget he is still there. It has happened to me, and in the end the surprise was still mutual, although for my ram it lasted only for a few seconds. Expertly mounted, that Stone ram reminds me forever of a time well spent, and a very good hunting companion to have spent the time with. What more can one hope for or expect from sheep hunting?

THE STORY OF LUCKY

1987 BC OUTDOORS

HE WAS A MOUNTAIN SHEEP, almost snow white except for his black muzzle, hooves and tail. His back was silvery gray. His horns were the color of amber and completely round in a full circle. He was born lucky.

The day he came into the world the May sun shone warm upon the rock shelf where his mother had birthed him. Only the previous day a late blizzard had shrieked over the bald mountain and threatened to blow mother and unborn lamb into the icy lake below.

Even so, he was lucky because his mother was old and wise in the ways of the Stone sheep. She had selected her lamb's birthplace with great care. It was a ledge of volcanic rock in the middle of a talus slope where only wild sheep can find good footing in times of danger. Facing the sun on the downhill side, the shelf was sheltered by a large boulder that was lodged solidly in the fine rubble above. The front was hidden by a large mountain juniper concealing the ewe and lamb from the prying eyes of a huge, ever hungry, golden eagle.

As he stood for the first time on his wobbly legs and nursed, his mother stood motionless, staring into the valley where a prospector panned for gold from the banks of the creek that tumbled gleaming from a spot up the mountains. The baby ram couldn't yet know how lucky he was. His mother nursed him with her rich, warm milk whenever he was hungry.

During the first cold nights when icy breezes whispered through the juniper branches, she would lay beside him warming his shivering body. But quickly his legs grew stronger. With this newfound strength he grew restless and playful. On his third day his mother led him back to the flock. Lucky bounced along like a little rubber ball. Under her expert care and guidance he quickly learned to use his legs on the secret trails where only mountain sheep can traverse.

She stood like a bulwark over him when the eagle swooped down threateningly. Another time a growling, slavering wolverine chased him into the loose rubble. The wolverine's sharp claws found nothing to grab but sand and pebbles. The little lamb was impossible to catch.

When winter came again, Lucky's mother led the flock onto a high plateau. Lucky was now protected by a thick fur coat and the winds blew away the snow, exposing forage for the sheep. During the late fall mating season, he met his father, Old MossHorn, and the other mature rams.

He was most impressed with their regal appearance. These proud old monarch's displayed a rather peculiar if not anti-social attitude toward the youngsters. Perhaps it was just their sense of humor that caused them to butt a young, inquisitive ram in the rump whenever he ventured too close. Alas, Lucky's pride was hurt on more than one occasion.

As time went by, his own horns grew in the characteristic curl of the Stone sheep. The first few years of his life were spent with the ewes and lambs playing and feeding on the nutritious grasses of his mountain home. In his fifth year he matured and the older rams allowed him to join their band that ranged apart from the females. His horns had grown into a three-quarter circle and he quickly learned the butting order. More than once he was butted to the rear of the troop.

His mother died during the following harsh winter. One day she simply lay down to rest, never to rise again. Lucky was not there to see her die. At the time he was eking out a meager living while traveling with the Rams on another mountain. Only during the following spring did he stumble upon her bleaching bones.

He ranged far afield, crossed many valleys and summits in search of safety, mates and food. He was now contemptuous of the eagle and the coyote – but never trusted the wolverine, timber wolf or lynx. He found if he stayed within easy distance of shale slides and steep slopes he was safe from four-legged predators.

Often the wolf pack lay waiting in ambush for him. Even a mountain grizzly had tried to catch him. Born on surefooted, springy legs, he always managed to bound away onto a cliff, usually amid the loose pile of rock and rubble where pursuit became difficult, if not impossible, for the hungry carnivores. He recognized the need for traveling bands because eight or 10 pairs of sharp eyes usually could spot danger sooner and more easily than only one.

It was in his ninth season. His horns had begun to grow their second curl and he became aware of a strange new enemy. He had on occasion only seen these two legged creatures climbing about the mountains, usually near creeks where they poked about the gravel. But these newcomers –- instinct told him –- were very different and dangerous to him.

He saw strange sticks on their backs or in their hands and sometimes he heard strange thunder echoing in the valleys. He heard the buzzing sound of apparently angry bees which occasionally buried themselves in the ground near him or struck the rocks. He remained lucky and unhurt, although he watched a few brothers fall, never to be seen again by the flock.

Year after year Lucky advanced in the butting order for the right to breed. He fathered many lambs and one season finally battled and defeated Old MossHorn who had been the acknowledged leader. Old MossHorn was too old now and was forced to abdicate his position. He became a loner and soon afterward fell victim to a pack of wolves. As leader of the column, the safety of the herd became Lucky's responsibility.

Nothing ever escaped his emerald green eyes. He could spot a crouching wolf a mile away by the nervous twitch of a tail tip. Once he spotted a lynx when it wrinkled its nose to test the wind. There were occasions when in spite of his watchful eyes, thunder struck from clear skies and another brother fell.

Many times now he has seen the same hunter. He had no real way of knowing this two legged creature's desire to possess his great flaring horns. He didn't realize how magnificent a specimen he had become.

The hunter knew of course. He had hunted far and wide at great expense and effort. He knew there wasn't another ram in those mountains with greater thorn growth than Lucky. For many seasons the same hunter had searched Lucky's home range but never managed to approach within accurate shooting distance.

In his 13th season, Lucky saw the hunter far away in the Valley tracking a moose. He didn't know that the hunter figured Lucky to be dead of old age. Searching for moose, the hunter came close to one of the mountain trails used by Lucky's flock. At the old prospector's cabin, the hunter rested after his arduous climb from his own lake shore camp. Under a canopy of blue Spruce, the shimmering aspen, and willows mixed with the scarlet of scrub birch, a light colored object moved through the trees attracting his attention.

At first the hunter thought it was a wolf or the white-maned neck of a bull caribou. Suddenly, there stood Lucky in all his regal magnificence – and mercifully unaware of the crosshairs settling on his heart region. No breeze brought the hunter's assent to his nostrils. No sound disturbed him so he grazed to within a few yards of his nemesis.

The hunter was excited. He held Lucky's life on the tip of his trigger finger. But he wrestled with his conscience and control his urge to kill. He was aware of the fact that Lucky had likely become expendable to the flock and that he no longer contributed to its growth and welfare. But he too, had learned much during a lifetime of hunting. His own heart had softened and his philosophy on life had mellowed. Quite inexplicably he reasoned that the ram had fulfilled his part in the mechanics of the universe and now deserved to live out his natural life in peace.

"Go on about your business!" He said softly, lowering his rifle.

Still unaware of the danger he has stumbled into, Lucky eventually followed his chosen trail. His head held high, he disappeared from the hunter's view forever.

The man was surprised by his own action and by the feeling of peace that had come over him with the decision to let this magnificent ram live another day. He felt more elated than he had in many a year. Winter came early that year. By September hard frosts had killed the juicy lupines and grasses upon which the sheep fed. There was only a little dry hay left on the stock and even it was soon covered by deep snow. By October the sheep had to dig deep to find sustenance.

They grew weaker by the day and when the breeding season came few rams had the strength to do battle for breeding rights. Lucky was not one of them because starvation, lung worms and other parasites had weakened him to the point of total exhaustion. One cold snow-blown day he stumbled along an old familiar trail and came to his birthplace.

He lay down to rest. Lucky watch the white world grow fuzzy. His body ached, yet he made no sound of complaint. Slowly, imperceptibly, his head sank to the frozen ground. One last steaming breath escaped from his black nostrils. His body had shivered from the onset of the great eternal cold and subsequently he lay still. Heavy snow covered him quickly and it was not until spring that ravens and coyotes found him.

But Lucky hadn't died in vain. Lucky lived on in the genes of his sons and daughters, some of whom were almost perfect replicas of this great magnificent ram. In time some of them would perish through carelessness or misadventure, or the cunning of predators, but a select few would live on and the flock would prosper.

Sitting in his comfortable home the hunter mused often about this wonderful great ram. He was glad he hadn't killed him. He really didn't need to possess his great horns to remind him of the many glorious days he has spent on Lucky's mountain.

It must be a poor soul indeed, he reasoned, who must depend on the measurements of a magnificent creature's horns published in some record book to gain some measure of prestige and immortality for himself. He, himself, had played God's role often enough. He too, was tired of the hunting game.

SURVIVING IN STYLE

WHEN IT COMES TO OUTDOOR food and survival, I prefer to live well and long. I have had this preference for years, dating back to a desperately hungry, bone chilling night in September, 1955, while camped on a mountain in the Cascades.

Lying awake on a pile of juniper branches beside a small, smoky fire, I didn't appreciate the beauty around me. An almost full moon climbed up the clear sky, illuminating the snowfields of Mount Coquihalla and the silvery waterfall to the south of us that dropped nearly 3000 feet (915 m) into the valley. While camping in shirt sleeves above timberline, with precious little fuel for a fire, we cursed the day we planned to hunt goats. On the tiny fire was a makeshift pot of tinfoil which contained our only ration of food: two cubes of chicken broth in melted snow.

In 1955, we were greenhorns. We knew little of hunting and nothing about cooking or nutrition, and even less of the art of comfortable alpine camping. In our defense, we never intended to climb such a high mountain, or to camp overnight. We simply got carried away by unlimited, unbridled, and therefore ignorant enthusiasm.

For my second goat hunt, my backpack according to the bathroom scales came in at 65 pounds (30 kg). I was so loaded down with gear I never made it up any mountain. An old suicidal (or foolish) billy goat met me half way. I didn't miss.

My "Trapper Nelson Pack board" was stuffed with goodies from the local delicatessen: fancy cheeses, salami's, butter, sourdough bread, soups, vegetables, canned meats, even Swiss chocolate. There was a space filled with the necessary cookware and an expensive sleeping robe. Tied to the whole works was a tent and an air mattress. My partner figured I had overdone it. By the looks of his pack – he had done the same.

We lived like kings from then on. Hunting and camping became enjoyable even though my first attempts at camp cooking ruined a lot of good food. To cook well out of doors in grit, grime, and flying ashes and bugs, requires more than mere talent. It requires dedication and perhaps a gluttonous craving for good food.

I once went on a backpack hunt for California Bighorn sheep with a bonafide survival expert. That fellow believed in traveling light. He laughed at me chugging up the steep trails like a leaky steam engine with a 65 pound pack.

By evening, we broke out of the timber and actually spotted a few sheep, but were too tired to go further. Behind a grassy knoll we pitched our camp. For lack of suitable fuel my friend collected dried cow dung for the fire.

I was a little more experienced by that time, so it was no great trick to heat the soup, and make corned beef – and mashed potatoes. With a can of asparagus and a tin of oranges for dessert it was a good meal.

Before the hunt, we had agreed we would be responsible for our own provisions. I had already finished my meal when I realized all my partner had consumed with a cup of coffee brewed in a rusty anti-freeze can he found. He had it hanging over the fire by some barbed wire liberated from a cattle drift fence.

He was a Spartan fellow. Aside from a little coffee he had brought nothing that I would consider edible. Had it not been for stories of his ability to live off the land, I might've fed him. I wanted to see just how long he could hold out.

At dawn he was up to light the fire. A strong wind blew cow chip ashes into his coffee pot, but he drank the stuff as if it were nectar from the gods.

I cooked my breakfast of smoke cured Westphalian ham, fried eggs with hash browns, and percolated clean coffee. His hungry eyes told me I was a genuine son of a bitch if I continued to let him starve any longer.

I did. To his credit he never asked for anything. At lunchtime however, I couldn't stand it when he literally counted every bite I took of bread and salami. I fed him. He ate like a horse.

During the past three seasons I have tasted the best and worst of camp cooking. At one camp, the camp cook used a cast-iron Dutch oven and put it in the coals of the fire pit. He filled it with beans, a little salted pork, water and some vegetables. At supper, he would dig it up and serve that unholy mess. Sometimes a grouse or a chunk of deer or bear meat was tossed into the pot with more beans and water "to add substance." Leftovers always remained in the pot. What a mess. I nearly cried every time a plump grouse was tossed into that devils' kettle.

After a week of eating this uninspired, nasty fare, fully aware that the first to complain would become the cook, I investigated the well-filled grub boxes. To my surprise they contained everything a hotel chef would want in his kitchen. It was just a case of laziness. I raise a little hell.

I didn't mind the cooking job; especially since one of my partners had killed a fat, young mule deer buck. I was hungry for steaks; for barbecued ribs; and Hungarian-style goulash. In one box I found a sack of apples, enough to go around; with some left over to be whittled into our pancake mix.

There was enough lettuce and greens to make tossed salads. We didn't eat another bean on that trip. The grouse the boys brought were browned in butter and steamed in their own juices with only a strip of bacon, and a diced onion added for each bird. Suddenly, it seemed that no one had liked the other fellow's cooking at all. It's true I spent a little less time hunting, but better food made for a happier crew.

Another time, on a planned fly-in trip with two partners, our pilot looked at our gear, and said it would take either a bigger aircraft, or two trips to get us where we were headed. We chartered a larger plane – a Beaver on floats. They flew in the whole lot of us, including my partner's beloved marshmallows for his hot chocolate. We lived comfortably through that wonderful experience – although we didn't kill a single game animal.

It was in sharp contrast to my first fly-in experience when two of us planned to live out of a light backpack while hunting stone sheep well above timberline. That was the only such trip I ever made without bringing a good cook stove. For three days I "cooked" the hydrated food using candles.

I called the whole thing off as a bad experiment gone wrong and we moved back down to the lake shore where we could find a little willow wood to cook on. From there we sat counting the days waiting for the plane to fetch us and deliver us to a good restaurant.

I gathered some of my most enjoyable culinary experiences while on a canoe trip on the southern half of Atlin Lake. It was in the days before certain hunting closures came into effect. We bagged a mountain goat which had to complete the journey back to camp while strapped to the canoe's outrigger. It became the cleanest, whitest goat I ever saw.

We also fished a lot for char. We didn't really need the well-filled grub box— but it was great insurance in case we had to wait out a storm or two. We fried the goat liver with a mess of fried onions, potatoes, and mushroom soup gravy.

At the southern end of the Llewellyn Inlet it rained hard. We camped in a simple lean-to right at the spot where the glacier trail begins. I remember it so well because neither of us got much sleep that night. A grizzly had scented our fish. He grunted and growled a lot, and vented his frustrations on some nearby trees and shrubs. Finally not really wanting a fight he wandered off into the inky night. Who can sleep at a time like that?

Once I cooked for European hunter who had been around the world a few times. I was cooking four fat Mallard ducks in a turkey pan with gravy. The gravy was made by taking a little onion soup mix, stirring in hot water, adding the vegetable oil in which the ducks were roasted. Onions were already in there. I added a little salt, pepper, garlic powder and a squirt of MAGGI for seasoning. Lastly, I added a can of diced mushrooms.

I heard no complaints from him. Especially not when I opened a fine bottle of wine and served it chilled with the duck dinner, scalloped potatoes, and green beans fried in butter and breadcrumbs.

I admit it doesn't necessarily make for a better hunter without the urgency to produce a kill for food – but outdoor living can be much more fun. The selective hunter is undoubtedly a safer and happier person to be on the trip with.

STUCK IN THE MUD MOOSE

1969

SITTING ON ONE OF OUR MANY gearboxes a grim faced Phil Myers chewed on the tough ptarmigan carcass I cooked for him.

"I just had a wonderful idea," he announced, "I plan on giving this pothole of a lake a proper name... something fitting that'll put it on the map for what it really is. I hate to see someone else make the same mistake of coming here to hunt moose as we did."

He leaned over the map that lay unfolded on the camp table and pointed at the tiny blue dot that looked so innocent and pretty among the green and brown lines of the Snowden range.

"Just look at it again," as he shoved the map over to me and continued, "it hasn't even been named yet. I suppose either nobody's had the guts to put a tag on this swamp... or else we are the first nitwits ever to come here."

"No-Catch-Em Lake" sound about right to you?" I asked.

With the last bite of ptarmigan safely chewed up and swallowed he muttered as if to himself but still audible enough to be meant for me.

"No moose, no caribou, no sheep, and no damn fish. We've come 1800 miles from Vancouver for nothing."

I didn't really blame Phil for being bitter and disappointed, although he hadn't hired me to guide him. Being my neighbor, I had taken it upon myself to show him some of British Columbia's better moose range. He'd never hunted anything larger than a duck.

When he asked if he could come along on this hunt I answered enthusiastically, "Sure! Why not?" I hinted at the possibilities of collecting a new world record trophy and we both laughed at that suggestion.

"Just charter that Beaver float plane and fly around the sourdough country," he spoke directly to me as he continued his lament.

"The trouble with you is that you're too damn optimistic just like the chairman of the Chamber of Commerce and the tourist bureau rolled into one. I bet a fellow couldn't even catch a social disease up here."

"Well now..." I couldn't let him get away with such a statement, "if that's what you're after, we will pack up here and I can find someone to take you on a guided tour of Vancouver's skid row."

"No. No. You know what I mean. In seven days of hard hunting we didn't find one single species of big game," as he heaved the ptarmigan skeleton into the fire. "Even these are impossible to chew on and tougher than a grizzly bear's hind quarters," he cussed.

Phil was only partly right because on our third day out I had a run-in with a mean she-wolverine and had to shoot the beast. Later we found a flock of Stone sheep but only a single three-quarter curl ram among them.

"He's too small to brag about," Phil had complained, "and besides I wouldn't want to be known as the guy who shot the last of the Stone's. Your wolverine is hardly bigger than a Keremeos chipmunk."

We searched the high ridges around the swamp for caribou but all we found was a large passel of ptarmigan.

"Suppose I can hunt them with my bow and arrows?" He asked.

"Sure I have no personal objections, if you have the right type of arrows and know how to use them," I replied.

The following morning he brought his hunting bow forth.

"65 pounds of pull," he explained. "And it won't even disturb other game."

His accuracy amazed me. The slender aluminum shafts drove straight and true. Although a ptarmigan is a rather small bird, Phil didn't miss. His first shot pierced about halfway through the bird and stuck fast. Not the ptarmigan though. It unwound in a flurry of feathers and wings and sailed off downhill. Halfway across the deep canyon it suddenly dropped dead. Phil wasn't discouraged at first. So he tried again with similar results. Finally he nailed a bird to a clump of moss. That's the one I cooked for him — and like he complained — it was tough.

"Damn expensive birds, too," he complained, "$2.95 per shot… wholesale that is."

While Phil studied the map I finished my supper. As I stuffed my pipe I glanced through our open tent flap and saw a splash of water down on the lake shore right where a small peninsula cut halfway across from the opposite shore. I reached for my binoculars.

"What are you looking at now?"

"There's a moose in the lake," I replied. After a second look, "There are two large animals in the water near the peninsula. Still want to call it No-Catch-Em Lake?"

"Yup. We haven't got one yet, have we?"

Phil busied himself with his big spotting scope.

"Holy smoke, there are three animals," he corrected. "But I can only see two of them clearly – they're both cows."

"The third must be a bull... want to go after him?"

Phil-tested the wind.

"It'll be dark in an hour," he said. "And that breeze is all wrong... it's blowing right from here to them. But, sure, why not? Let's go after them."

He rummaged among his gear and broke out his chest-high fishing waders and while I inflated our rubber boat he put them on.

"We'll need the axe and some rope too," he reminded me. "And don't forget the lantern because we might have to skin that moose by gaslight."

Originally Phil had planned to hunt moose with his fibreglass bow but I convinced him to take his rifle along. I just didn't like the idea of having a bunch of razor sharp broad headed arrows in our fragile rubber boat.

"Take lots of shells along," I said.

There was only one chance to approach the moose and this meant we had to cross the lake and then row or drift down on them and hope they wouldn't catch our scent.

The dinghy rolled and twisted like a tired old jellyfish.

"Faster," Phil urged, "Much faster or it will be too dark for me get a shot in there."

I knew a trapper had once cut a trail around the mile-long lake but the willow bush had grown dense again and the beavers had since damned the surrounding swamps so that its water level was nearly 3 feet higher than the lake itself.

Resting in the boat's stern, Phil was awfully impatient.

"Hurry it up! Get this phony bathtub moving!"

I allowed myself a glance over my shoulder to see how far we would have to go.

"Better lay down," I advised him. "If the moose sees one wrong movement they'll all take off. With a little luck the wind will drift us right to the peninsula and we'll have cover there. We can just get out and blast him."

"I'll do the shooting," Phil said. "Remember old boy, you told me you just wanted a caribou – this moose is mine!"

The sun had just dipped behind the snowy ridges of the Snowden Range to our left. I knew we'd have to hurry. Hugging the shoreline on our right I hoped our silhouettes might blend with the willows of the swamp I rowed again.

"For goodness sakes be careful," Phil complained, "don't splash so damn much! The moose will hear you."

"That figures!" I thought. "This is his first big game hunt and he sounds like an expert already."

"You're sure it'll be a bull?" he inquired.

"It better be. I hate to row you around the lake just for the fun of it. Can you see him yet?"

"Yeah. There's something black moving about the bushes on the far shore. It's coming into the lake now. There are ripples on the water. Now there's something white way up over its back. What is that?"

I stole another glance over my shoulder and my heart stopped for a moment. That "**something black**" was indeed the greatest bull moose I had ever seen. He stood ankle deep in the lake and looked like a black Clydesdale plow horse wearing a halo. His huge antlers shone like the white of a Dall sheep.

Gravel scraped the frail bottom of our boat so we scrambled in knee-deep water and pulled it up into the bushes of the peninsula.

"Hey, how come he hasn't seen us?"

"He must be watching the cows," I replied.

"There he is again. Say... are you sure it is a bull... all that white stuff on its back. Shouldn't we get closer?"

I still hadn't recognized him for what he was but the bull waded out toward us. It seemed as if he wanted to join the feeding cows. I peeked through the bush to check on the cows and sure enough they had their heads under water feeding on lily roots.

Just then one cow looked up and saw us. In a flash, the water exploded into foam. Half running and half swimming she headed for the swamp.

The bull moved too. He had grown to such a gigantic size by avoiding hunters. He stepped mighty high and fancy to reach for cover.

Phil finally recognized him and he shivered with excitement.

"Whoa! Hold off a second!" I shouted at him. "You can't shoot while he is still in the lake! Hang on –- now!"

But it was too late! Phil stood a little behind me and to my left and the muzzle blast of his magnum nearly blew my ears off.

"He's down," Phil hollered.

The bull had fallen onto his haunches. In the shower of water and mud he turned over onto his back. He struggled for a moment but regained his footing.

"Shoot!" I hollered. And promptly another blast pounded my eardrums.

The bull staggered and fell but in a flash he was up again. Phil had missed that time and his bullet had hit the water. I saw it ricochet into the beaver dam.

Another flash and blast and again the bull fell. The whomp of a solid hit echoed across the lake. The bull was in real trouble now and he struggled to get up. He shoveled water and mud with his broad antlers and he sat up like a big dog. Phil's fourth shot brought him down again.

Poor damn moose, I thought. "Put that poor thing out of its misery! Take better aim next time and kill him cleanly!"

"I can't..." Phil's voice was all choked up and his face looked sadder than a basket full of basset hounds. "I have no more shells."

"Take my rifle," I told him. "Hold dead on this time. You wanted that moose so you better finish him now."

He grabbed my old Mauser and raised it to his shoulder and lowered it again.

"No. I can't shoot with iron sights. You better do it," as he handed the rifle back to me.

Miraculously the bull had regained his composure. Three good strides carried his hulk to the beaver dam. He scrambled to gain its summit when my sights settled on his massive neck. The muzzle flash blinded me for an instant and when I could see again the moose had disappeared.

"Look who's doing all the shouting. You can miss too, huh?" The biggest damn moose in the world and my 'expert' partner let him get away. What a magnificent creature!"

"Where in the hell did you aim at?" I asked.

Every day since we have gone on this trip Phil had asked me where he should aim. At least a dozen times I told him to shoot for the heart or the neck for a quick humane kill.

"Right in the middle," he replied. "I th…th…thought…" he stuttered embarrassed, "that my .375 caliber Magnum would knock him over for keeps!"

"He didn't get away," I interrupted him. "He's got to be down right behind the dam. Let's get the boat over there."

While I rowed Phil readied the gas lantern.

"We'll skin and quarter him tonight and tomorrow will bring out the trophy and the meat," I said.

"You think he'll hold still long enough?" Was his reply.

I brought the boat to shore downwind of the moose.

"Just in case he is still alive... **do not** make any noise," I whispered.

"This is stupid," I reminded myself and Phil. "With all these mud holes, water and hummocks – if he's still alive he can charge us and we can't even get out of his way."

Phil lit the lantern and tied it to a very long, dry, willow pole. Holding it high in front of him an eerie light flickered and danced through the swamp.

"I trust we aren't breaking any laws," he whispered, "hunting with a light like this?"

"I hate to do it too," I replied. "But it's not hunting. I'm just trying to find and skin the moose."

The swamp waters gurgled and swished about our feet. I thought Phil was lucky to be wearing his chest waders. Jumping and skating, every step was a struggle on the slippery footing of the spongy hummocks. We searched the area as best we could.

A big splash startled me and I jerked around pointing my rifle automatically. It was Phil. He'd missed a step and fallen into a hole. I cast the end of my rope to him and dragged him out. Thanks to his waders he had remained dry. But the expensive rifle he still carried was soaked in slime and mud.

Our lantern still burned bright and hadn't suffered in the fall. We struggled another dozen steps forward and Phil called out. "Hey... look! See that white thing there in the middle of the big puddle?" He held the lantern way out over the bog."

"No, I guess it's probably just an old antler. These moose travel right through the middle of muck. They aren't too fussy where the drop their used headgear."

The bog was too large to get close enough for a discriminating examination of the antler but it seemed somewhat attached to something that looked very much like a muskrat house. I noticed the 3 to 4 inches of surface water was quite muddy with reddish streaks flowing through it. Air bubbles rose to the surface and burst all around the platform. The antler moved. Phil noticed it too.

"Hey, look again. That old horn's sinking. I bet you shot it clean off the old bull. I'll be damned that shovel must be at least 3 feet long."

Suddenly he sensed the tragic truth and lurched ahead to save the antlers. I grabbed him by the coat sleeve just in time.

"Whoa! You can't go in there. If a whole moose can disappear in that bog – so can you! Let it go – we're too late now!"

"You mean my moose is still on that horn?"

I nodded.

"Well, help me get it out! We've got to do something. We just have to!" He stuttered helplessly. "How about a rope? We can tie it to the horns and hold the moose up. We'll tie it to a tree or something."

He reached for the rope as I gave it to him. Fumbling, nervously, he fashioned a loop and cast for the antler. On his second try the rope draped itself around the great shovel.

"Don't just stand there! Help me! Come on I've got it!" He struggled with all the strength of his 6 foot frame.

"For Christ sakes help me!" He yelled.

The rope was 30 feet long. I knew it and I had already looked around for an anchor tree but there was nothing close enough.

Phil struggled like a man possessed. He had stuck the lamp pole into the mud so he could have both hands free. Sweat rolled off his forehead and for a moment he seemed to win. Carried away by his excitement I reached over to help him pull. Slowly the other antler rose from the mire and for the first time we saw the huge trophy close-up.

"That's a 6 foot spread," Phil groaned. "We gotta save it."

Urged by a wild and desperate desire he pulled the rope with a grizzly bear's strength.

Splash!!!

The inevitable happened. Our hummock footing collapsed suddenly and we both fell into the mud. I reach for a handful of willow branches on the way down and pulled myself out. I was filthy dirty but Phil was in desperate shape. He had fallen backwards and lost his grip on the rope. His chest waders had filled with water and the black mud oozed into them to and he settled down into the bog.

There was no time to waste. In my hurry to save him I couldn't find the loose ends of the rope. I reached out over the bog and cut off as much rope as I could gather from what was on the antlers of this moose and tossed it to Phil. We both struggled with the sucking muck.

"Careful!" he yelled. "You're yanking me right out of my pants."

And so it happened. Wet, bare and cold, I struggled to get Phil back to our camp. The moose was lost for good.

Later that night after we cleaned up and enjoyed the beneficial effects of a hot and strong beverage, Phil sat down to brood over his lost trophy.

"Damn it all, I wouldn't have guessed it. So much bad luck. And who'd believe me back home? It was such a great bull and might've been a new world record, you know."

"It's all your own fault," I replied. "You put a jinx on this place and that poor moose. You shouldn't have called it No-Catch-Em Lake.

P.S. I never hunted with him again.

THE IDEAL DUCK PUNT MEANS BETTER HUNTING

Henry E. Prante

JULY 1965 NW SPORTSMAN

The value of a good duck punt is not obvious to most folks. Its virtues and potentials I find must endure more detailed investigation and explanation if the average waterfowl hunter is to receive all the benefits of its use. To hunt waterfall isn't art these days. It requires special skills, equipment and knowledge.

Not-so-experienced hunters and ammunition manufacturers tell me that the good old days of scattered gunning are gone. They say I need particular brands of powder and shot for my old gas pipe and that I have to practice with Clay targets to increase my efficiency at killing birds I want to eat.

Other well-meaning contemporaries want me to use certain gumboots or shooting jackets to help me fill my game bag. Those boys do make their point, but I like to add hard-earned information and data.

First off, it isn't nearly as hard to find good hunting as some old timers try to tell you. How else could they possibly shoot their limits and most of them do? They do know, of course, how to close the gap between gun muzzle and the bird before they pull the trigger. That's where this most important gadget, the duck punt, receives its place of honor. Without it the jazziest outfit may prove useless.

Last winter, Ed made asked me to design and build the ideal duck punt. Ideal for him, he'd said, and for the prevailing conditions in the Fraser River Delta. Now let's take a close look at Ed's idea and you'll see what a Hunter with many years of experience to his credit, considers necessary and appropriate for the worthwhile game of waterfowling.

"12 feet long should be about right," he told me, "and a beam of 38 inches would be maximum. It shouldn't draw more than 2 to 3 inches of water while fully loaded and have a proper trounce some where I can mount my three-horse outboard motor: a safe boat without too much freeboard."

While there you are. At first I thought Ed expressed rather excessive demands and that such a craft could never be built. But after further conversation with him I became aware of the special, sometimes outstanding qualities of good duck punt. He told of his old Bicknell punt, for instance, which had performed well with those approximate dimensions. But that he now preferred square stern for easy motor mounting and that it was now because his old one is too heavy for him alone to handle easily.

"I'm not as young as I would like to be," he said. "When you want your old pals get laid flat by heart failures he began to sink in reasonable terms. You suddenly convince yourself that you deserve better — much better than to die of overexertion — wrestling upon to and fro."

Judging from personal observation I venture to claim that most of the expert duck shooters hereabouts are on the wrong side of middle age. This can easily be explained by enthusiasm for the sport, a long apprenticeship, and determination to stick with it and to hunt just one more season.

Younger hunters, like me for instance, usually learned the hard way by stumbling through the mud for a few seasons without encouraging results. Some give up ducks forever then that while others somehow learned the tricks of waterfowling. After which follows the joy that only a full bag limit can bring to the hunter's heart.

Perhaps you too, have found it strange and confusing that punts like other types of boats come in a large variety of shapes and forms and have asked yourself: is there really a need for different models? Why should some be better than others, and what exactly are the desirable virtues and the duck punt?

I'm sure these and many other questions have confused would-be duck hunters, including your correspondent. I have built many boats in the past, from fast little roundabouts to racing Halls, and then a number of those glossy elaborate headaches that only millionaires can afford. I had always been confident that I could build a little punt for sure. Then I became interested in scatter guns and right away loss two good hunters over the side of the wrong type of punt. This slowed me down considerably, but I still wanted to hunt birds.

But duck shooting friend of mine once defined the duck punt as a cross between an Eskimo's kayak and an Indian canoe. It must be stable, light in weight, and easy to maneuver in the treacherous currents of our saltwater marshes.

Like its enthusiastic owner, it must withstand the racing ways of the Gulf when a Sou'wester drives rain and hail stones like pitchforks, and the honkers must buck the gale to reach their feeding grounds. It may perhaps be similar to a Louisiana-Swamp-Whatchamacallit like they might use in Duck Dynasty today. (Duck Dynasty wasn't around when this article was written or this punt built.) But it should never be like the roundabouts and frowns or the odd hydroplanes that now and then chased ducks and geese from Point Grey to Boundary Bay.

I've watched those makeshift punts many times. Usually they aren't doing too well. But every season someone has an idea and tries his best to catch a bird or two.

A number of years ago a good friend of mine hunted Canada geese on a farm near off Oshawa, Ontario. Thousands of the great birds used a nearby lake as a resting spot in their southward migration.

"They always managed to stay out of range," my friend told me. "I nearly went crazy with frustration. I noticed that their flight beacon nearly always lead them right over our huge barn, still out of range mind you. Then one day I had an idea and climbed onto the roof of that barn and hid behind a ventilation housing. Man, did those geese ever learn the hard way. I got my limit every day until the migration was over."

Incidents like that prove that a waterfall gunner must use his imagination and ingenuity. While a barn can serve as a shooting platform in some places, they are hard to find in a marsh. A duck punt is the only ticket to successful hunting there.

Bearing all these facts in mind I set to work on Ed's punt. I must confess that throughout the designing and construction. I felt a good measure of anxiety wondering how it would turn out.

Seaworthiness, stability with a full load, either under power in deep water, or while being poled along through the shallows is of prime importance in a punt. But to combine those features with spaciousness and comfort for the hunter in an ultralight, easily concealable craft, it is a very tall order indeed. To complicate matters further NNI wanted to use reasonably priced materials and drew up the plans so the average home builder can read them and perhaps benefit by building his own. Ed had a set a weight limit to the project at approximately 70 to 80 pounds maximum. The plans and full instructions to this duck punt are available via Amazon and Kindle.

I think it is important to mention here that this punt is a one-man boat. I've heard of cases where two hunters crowded together for economic reasons and then, in the sometimes furious action and excitement shot each other. It takes considerable discipline by both partners to make a two-man punt work out all right. To begin with a much larger craft is required and this in turn commands the use of costlier materials — besides — the larger the punt the harder it will be to conceal it.

It is a well-known fact that ducks and foul weather go together like a long winter swim and ammonia. Perfect combinations, don't you think? Still the good punt must be serviceable under those conditions. When water safety experts tell the public not to stand up in the small craft the duck hunter is the exception. He must pull this punt through the shallows where he isn't likely to lose his life right away, but where he often has to jump the birds before he can shoot, and then his craft must be stable enough to allow accuracy — without dumping him into the water.

And other times a conspiracy of river currents, high tides, and gale force winds work against the Hunter. This usually occurs when he has to cross a wide stretch of open water to reach a particular feeding ground, or after a hard day of hunting and he is tired.

I remember a time when the late Rudy Schultheiss and I chased a crippled snow goose from Sea Island halfway across the Gulf of Georgia. We had no motor on our punt so we never caught the goose. I fair wind came up instead and I swear that no two other fellows ever paddled harder and were more scared than both of us. Many anxious hours passed before we reached home again.

Power-drive for the hunt that is primarily used on rivers or entitled waters must be considered essential. The punt, at least, should have provisions for easy mounting of a no board motor. Some of the maximum tides occur from November to March when the waterfowling is at its best. Two bucks such tides combined with river currents is not only tiring but sometimes extremely dangerous.

It feels good to sit back and let the little egg beater do all the work. Our hunting regulations won't permit anyone to shoot from any power bull while underway, but once the engine is shut off, and the punt is at anchor, it becomes legal again. The best choice of power is up to and including the 3 hp in the popular models. Larger engines are much too bulky and too powerful, thereby defeating the purpose of the light punt.

Decoys are usually credited with bringing the birds into effect if shooting range and rightly so, however, you can bet your last bean, on opening morning of the season no self-respecting duck or goose will come within 100 yards of them if you and your punt are visible. You must conceal yourself and blend into the surroundings. You need to look as innocent as a piece of drift wood or a patch of weeds — but never be a flashy show off.

Don't forget that load of decoys that are very necessary indeed, but depending upon the area and weather conditions, they can mean a bulky cargo. Here in the Pacific Northwest a single hunter might use as many as 75 blocks in one set.

Camouflage is the magic cloak of any successful bird shoot. Decent duck hunters must operate from its folds to be successful. In some areas one may dig pits. While in others even heated wooden blinds are used to fool the birds. Alas, the Hunter of the marshes is usually stuck with this punt as he must depend upon it to furnish both transportation and hide out. Currents and tides often make it impossible to dig in, or else affect the feeding patterns of the birds. This requires the hunter to move his hideout often.

The simplest way to provide cover for Ed's punt was to drill holes into the gunwale rails at about 6 inch centers and plug-in bundles of grass. This method will allow him to change his colors as the circumstances may demand. I kept the camouflage rack below at the gunwale and close to the water line.

One can have a dry cockpit by installing splashrails or coamings around it. It will add to the free board, but since it is well inside the blind, this doesn't disturb the birds. I canvas cover can be installed over the whole cockpit area to help keep the water out and the hunter warm. Not long ago I met a chap who used the catalytic heater under such a cover. He claims it works very well.

After Ed's first hunt with his new Marsh Fox duck punt I was amazed to watch them unload his limit of eight beautiful birds, but was absolutely flabbergasted when I saw his gun. He had killed his birds with a tiny 20gauge autoloader. This was at a time when gun makers advocated the use of magnums on anything from butterflies to crocodiles.

"It's easy," Ed replied with a smile. "If you make them come to you!"

P.S. The plans and instructions are available in print on Amazon in the Workshop Series or Kindle.

THE ART OF TRACKING GAME

WHEREVER AND WHENEVER HUNTERS gather, one can usually hear talk of tracks and tracking wild animals. In fact, a novice overhearing such talk will probably be inclined to believe that they are privileged to hear some rare and awe inspiring testimony.

This happened to me some 40 odd years ago. I often heard phrases such as "…the buck's tracks were still smokin' hot", or "those tracks couldn't have been fresher if he still stood in them." This is picturesque and inspirational chatter alright, but I also learned that few folks had much use for cold tracks.

Reality is even more confusing. However, the honest-to-goodness art of tracking wild animals is often not mastered by the weekend warrior type of nimrod. To find a fresh track… correctly identify it… determine its age with reasonable accuracy… follow it faithfully over hill and dale … dry ground or swamp… rocks… moss… or carpets of pine needles… and eventually catch up with its maker… well… it's about as difficult as trying to make love to an unwilling bear while standing up in a canoe… without a stabilizer like my pontoon. This is work for experts, indeed.

I vividly recall a hunt for white-tailed deer with two keen weekend sportsmen who were thoroughly confused by the multitude of tracks, and the apparent absence of their creators.

It had been raining and the ground was wet. I remember how the boys cussed when they found it impossible to unravel the maze of tracks or even find one that was still 'smokin'.

I too, thought it might have helped a great deal if those tracks had smoked, or at least sizzled bit. Alas, they sure didn't. We could be reasonably sure they were white-tailed tracks, because in that particular area deer will not come off the high ranges until snow drives them down. Of course, by their size one could easily determine which was adult or fawn. However determining the difference between the buck and doe tracks – was an impossibility.

With some hindsight and looking at this problem scientifically...I suppose there might have been some differences that escaped us. Perhaps a Native of North America with a lifetime of dependency upon the land, and much practise in these matters might've been able to sort things out. Unfortunately for us we had no such expert available.

During my years of hunting all species of North American games I have sincerely tried to master this art – if only to satisfy my curiosity and improve my hunting success. I have also learned that very few sport hunters can tell apart the tracks of our three B.C. deer species when compared to those made by wild or domestic pigs, goats, and sheep.

It stands to reason, the sport hunter simply never had to acquire the necessary skills and therefore few of them did. Indeed, tracks are not always what they seem to be to the eager hunter. There are smallish doe's with large feet who leave footprints like a four-point buck and vice versa.

I don't suggest here that every hunter must be an expert tracker to be successful. On the contrary. One is however, well advised to get an idea of how difficult tracking really can be. For example take a look at police work where a footprint in somebody's flower bed (one of the easier places) is the only clue a burglar left behind. Make no mistake about it – tracking is tracking – regardless of the different species or variety.

To find the culprit, the cops would likely bring into play a whole army of experts in hope of making a positive identification. They would likely enlist the services of soil experts, the weather office, meteorologists, shoemakers, or orthopedic specialists or surgeons perhaps. They would surely consult with makers of plastic or rubber footwear, in addition to chemists and other laboratory staff. Still with all that high-priced help working overtime – success is not automatic or guaranteed. But things have greatly improved over recent years with respect to new forensic police techniques.

All the elements of detective work are certainly present and applicable. It just simply depends on how serious you want to be. Many hunters, for the most part, don't take their sport very seriously – they depend largely upon luck.

Once, while hunting mule deer on horseback, I had the good fortune of bagging a fair-sized trophy buck. Leading my horse back down the trail to the ranch where my partner and I were staying – we came upon two saddled horses tied to a tree. They belonged to a pair of hunters, who likely had chosen to follow a game trail on foot. There was a whiff of snow on the ground and the rider's footprints showed as much. My partner, practical joker that he is, suggested we play a little trick on those hunters.

"Cut me a pair of 8 foot long sticks," he ordered, pointing to a nearby willow bush. "I'll trim a pair of feet off your buck and lace them to the sticks. I'll ride around slowly with the horses and poke lots of deer tracks into the snow. That ought to get those hunters quite excited don't you think?"

"Why not," I replied and started whittling the sticks. It seemed a great idea at the time and good for a laugh. So we did the dirty deed before returning to the bunkhouse.

Late that night two tired, but excited nimrods – strangers to us – came in to share the facilities. They had seen my buck hanging outside and related how they had 'goofed' up.

"No, we haven't gotten our deer yet, but tomorrow we should get lucky. Just imagine – if only we had stayed with our horses today, instead of leaving them tied out. It looks like, a whole herd of deer must've surrounded the poor old nags where the stood. Smoking hot tracks everywhere! We'll go back there in the morning!"

The two guys were bigger than us… so it was perhaps appropriate punishment for us that we couldn't disclose our secret or laugh out loud. But, we decided to follow them in the morning to see what they would do.

It was hilariously funny. They tied their horses as before, but this time they sat on the horses backs with rifles at the ready, waiting for the deer to return. Naturally, we stayed clear.

Sometimes it's not difficult spotting a trail that leads through a dew-fresh meadow. Nevertheless, one must usually guess at what kind of animal has passed through. Was it a deer, elk perhaps, or just a Hereford cow? It has been my experience that only on occasion can a greenhorn hunter identify such trails accurately.

The easiest tracks are probably a bear's footprint in soft ground – and grizzly tracks in particular. The hoof prints of moose are often confused with cattle tracks – especially by a hunter who has never seen them before – and doesn't realize how long the stride of a moose really is. Elk can lay similarly confusing signs, while caribou and cattle seem to have more in common – except – few caribou are ever found on the cattle range.

A number of years ago I was asked to guide a party of sportsmen – including my own boss – on a late-season moose hunt – after a fresh fall of snow.

We were driving through open range country when my boss spotted a whole passel of fresh tracks along the road. It was fresh powdery snow the kind that doesn't leave clear prints.

Used to giving orders he demanded I stop the car. He organized what he called "a drive to round up those moose!"

When everybody was gone to follow the tracks that lead into a jack-pine forest, I returned to the car to wait for their return in comfort. Two hours later the gang showed up again with discouraged looks on their faces.

"Did you find those damn range horses?" I asked. But I quickly realized I shouldn't have asked that question because everybody became very angry with me. It became quite clear to me that it was a mistake to be a smart aleck within that hunting party.

When considering some expert tracker's testimony, I always recall some true incidents that happened in 1947-1948 in West Germany's Lower Saxony province, and not far from the city of Hannover where I used to live.

At the time a lot of domestic livestock was being destroyed inside their fenced pastures. This animal managed to remain unidentified for quite some time.

This case attracted many experts because literally hundreds of expensive cattle and sheep fell prey to the mysterious beast. Everyone was baffled and made many conflicting statements to the press who reported almost daily all the new misdeeds of this as yet, unidentified creature.

Finally, one inspired pundit, for want of an accurate identification dubbed it: 'Der Wuerger von Lichtenmoor'. That handle took. In English it translates to 'The Strangler of Lichtenmoor'. It was seen as a creature as mysterious as a cross between the 'Hound of the Baskerville's' and 'Jack the Ripper'. Speculation ran a mock.

Many 'so-called' experienced, big game hunters, came from afar to look at the grisly evidence and footprints. Some of them had experience on all continents, and consequently, their conjectures and speculations also ranged as far apart.

Some thought it was a large Australian dingo. Some figured only a lion or tiger could have done this type of damage. Even the lowly hyena was suspected. Since none of the suspected killers are native to Germany – traveling circuses and even zoos – were checked for lost or missing predatory animals.

All that speculation ended dramatically one moonlit night, when a farmer hell bent on protecting his livestock, climbed up into a tree blind that overlooked his pastures. In the moonlight he spotted a beast stalking his flocks. He was an excellent marksman and dropped the animal dead in its tracks.

It turned out to be a large European wolf. Needless to say – much prestige was lost that night while the farmer gained considerable status as a dangerous game hunter. His picture was in every paper the following day.

While driving in a snowstorm, through some fine deer and elk country within the Rocky Mountains range of British Columbia, two friends of mine also pondered tracking questions.

"This is most definitely excellent fresh tracking weather!" they concluded.

Suddenly as if on command, a white-tail buck popped up from the roadside thickets only 30 paces ahead of us. He stood there as if completely unconcerned about his future. I stopped the car of course – but continued our previous conversation by stating that here, for once, was at least a fresh track – albeit not 'smoking hot' – and I suggested they should get out of the car and at least take a good look at it.

When the car's doors opened the buck vanished with a great leap into some Christmas trees… but the boys were hot on his trail. I too, loaded my rifle, and waited right there. About 10 minutes passed and the buck returned on his old trail, just as I had expected he might. It was an easy shot and I dropped him.

Two hours later, in the dark, my friends return. They had somehow lost the buck's trail in 6 inches of fresh snow. They had found more tracks, followed them for a while, and eventually had trouble finding their way back to the road, and the car. They hadn't heard my shot.

Tracks sometimes include other evidence of animal activity such as feeding. It can be seen in the form of cut twigs, torn branches, or droppings – although the latter are often referred to – as 'sign' or 'spoor'.

Many years ago I had a friendly argument over just such 'signage' which was presumably deposited by an elk. A partner of mine went so far as to collect a hatful of brown, oblong pellets, just to convince me that elk actually ranged through this particular stretch of real estate.

At the time I thought he was perhaps a little crazy. But later on he had those droppings analyzed. He was informed they originated from a moose – but they were quite similar to elk species – if somewhat smaller in size.

My late friend and hunting partner Maximilian Winkler, of Richmond, British Columbia once summed up my own feelings about tracks, trail, and signage, after a hard day's hunt for deer in the Chilcotin country of B.C. Another partner had brought and heated lentil soup for supper and Max was spooning it passed bristly mustache. The soup was fortified with lots of plump little sausages that resembled elk spoor.

Max soon came across one of these tasty morsels. "Hrumph," he growled amiably while taking his soup bowl closer to the lantern to inspect his find. "Close to 50 years I have hunted in this country – I reckon I must've passed tons of this stuff lying about in the bush – BUT I had no idea it tasted this good!"

Seriously speaking now, I drew the conclusion that I had better be mighty observant, inquisitive, and careful when out in the wilderness, and never ever mix up any trails, tracks, signs, and little lumps that may look good enough to eat raw or in a soup.

THE DAY THE WOLVES HOWLED

1990

SOME OF LIFE'S EXPERIENCES may be forgettable regardless of how intense it may have been. One experience of mine, however, is not. It will remain etched in my memory forever. Five cerebral strokes have not been able to erase it. Age has not dimmed it – and as far as I'm concerned – it can remain with me throughout all eternity.

This experience began one September morning in 1978 at about 5 a.m. It has haunted me ever since. My partner and I had just set up a moose hunting camp on the lonesome shores of British

Columbia's Gladys Lake. This is about 35 air miles east of Atlin and 5 miles south of the Yukon border. The weather was gorgeous and sunny during the day with clear nights under brilliant displays of the aurora borealis. We were in a hunter's paradise because moose were plentiful and the fishing exceptionally good. We savoured every minute of our stay.

During our third night here as we were sleeping in our camper vehicle something woke me. I had no idea what it was so I just rolled over in my bunk, looked at my watch, intending to go back to sleep again. Suddenly I heard it. Wild, strange, and loud.

It was close to us and the sound sent shivers up and down my spine. Goosebumps erupted up and down my arms and legs. I don't frighten easily, and even this morning, it wasn't fright that caused me to shiver inside my warm bed. Rather it was the ancient call of the wild that stirred my feelings right to the marrow of my bones.

"Auuhhhh..." it howled through the chilly predawn."Aauhhhh!"

This howl was repeated by another half dozen other primitive throats. The echo reverberated from the hills behind our camp and from the mountains across the lake and gave me the feeling of being trapped inside a giant, stereo, echo chamber.

My partner finally awoke with a start. "What's that? What's happening?"

He jumped from his bed to look out of the windows and the chorus began anew. These chilling sounds came from very close range. In time

I could recognize individual voices within that chorus. Specifically one slightly higher pitched voice which broke constantly and ended each howl with "Aauhhh…ooh…ooh…uh…uh"

I was fascinated and peeked through the window but there was nothing to be seen. Thick fog hid the closest trees, and the lake shore which was only a few feet away was also invisible to us.

"What's going on?" My partner questioned again. He was new to the north country and I suppose was worried about his safety. He wouldn't openly say it, but he still grabbed his hunting rifle and held it tighter than he might have held onto a lover. Finally he seemed to recognize who the singers were. "Wolves, eh"?

I nodded. Indeed they were. A whole pack of them. At that moment I don't believe I would have fancied to step outside even for a minute. They must have been hunting because between howls I could hear their heavy breathing.

"What are we going to do now?" Asked my partner. "I don't suppose it would be safe to leave the camper now. Those wolves might attack us."

"As far as I'm concerned – I'm sure they won't be doing that – because I'm not going out there right now to find out!" I replied.

For a while we sat and smoked our pipes while the music played on. We tried to identify the voices and eventually figured there were at least a dozen animals outside.

"Why do they hang around? Do you think they want something from us? I mean… they must know we're in here!"

"Go ask them!" I responded. "My guess is that they're hunting the same moose we're after. With a little luck they'll have chased every moose in the area into the swamp or the lake. Exactly where we want them to be. Hunting from the canoe should be easy today."

"If they'll let us out of this camper!" was his hesitant reply.

"Just sit still for a while, and enjoy the serenade! Not many people ever get serenaded by a pack of wolves. Maybe we're special to them, eh? "

It was nearly 9 a.m. when the fog began to lift. I made a pot of coffee and cooked a light breakfast of scrambled eggs and toast and fed my partner in bed. The wolves were still in the area – still howling – but they managed stay out of sight.

Gladys Lake was still shrouded in a white mist as we paddled our canoe into the fog. I knew this country from previous visits and steered the canoe on the appropriate compass bearing to reach a channel that led to a swamp and another small lake where we had previously fished.

It had been extremely difficult to coax my partner out of the camper this morning. Finally with his rifle in one hand and a shotgun in the other he ran to the canoe. Once out on the water he began to relax.

"But what are we doing out here?" He asked. "We can't see a thing!"

"The fog is already lifting?" I responded. When it finally lifts all the way I want to be where the moose are and surprise them!"

With little difficulty we found the entrance to the channel. The sun was visible as a faint white disc on the eastern horizon. Suddenly my partner stopped his paddling. He pointed straight ahead.

A cow moose and her calf were in the water straight ahead of us. Their heads were underwater as they fed on lush vegetation. We passed them at 10 yards and carried on. The wolves continued to howl and seemed to have this whole swamp surrounded now.

From this point on I knew the swamp well. Only a moose could get through it on foot. Wolves would never have a chance to catch a moose in it. Suddenly though, I had the very eerie, unsettling feeling that the wolves were actually using us as their hunting dogs. I said as much to my partner.

"No. I doubt they're that smart!" he responded.

But, I pondered the possibility now that he'd mentioned it. If we chased some game out of the swamp where could it go? To precisely where the wolves were waiting, of course. That realization abruptly changed my attitude. I didn't need a moose so badly that I would allow a pack of wolves to use me to get their breakfast.

Ever so slowly the mist rose. Occasionally we frightened ducks off our course with the odd quack-quack to be heard… the occasional tail slap of a beaver upon the still water... and a guttural grunt from an invisible bull moose.

The channel wasn't deep. Three feet perhaps – but its water was crystal clear. Only by observing the bottom could we divulge that we actually moved as we paddled.

Suddenly the fog bank opened and right in front of us, sitting upon the clear blue water were thirteen swans. They were so busy preening themselves for the long flight south they reminded me of a stage full of ballerina's in a beautiful dance scene.

Our paddles, silent as they were, stopped completely. We sat motionless, faintly hidden by the mist, watching the swans' debut of the morning. Alas, like all great pleasures on earth, this show didn't last quite long enough. A couple of minutes perhaps went by, and one bird spotted us and gave a gentle warning to the others.

Instantly thirteeen pairs of eyes focused on us. They prepared to fly, running along the water's surface to get air under their huge wings. A minute later they disappeared from view. Only a few feathers drifted forlornly upon the crystal blue water. A large splash of water commanded our attention. A bull moose and his lady friend stood knee-deep on the water's edge and observed us motionlessly.

My partner reached for his rifle. Suddenly, without speaking a word, he put it down again. I didn't mind and was quite surprised at myself. At this moment hunting no longer mattered to me. A shot would've ruined the magic of this beautiful morning. There was no dire need to kill because our food boxes in the camper were still well-stocked. There would be other days to hunt.

    The sun won its battle with the mist and shone brightly over this pristine, wilderness paradise. Silently we paddled back to camp. All the wolves were silent except for the one with the 'junior' voice who couldn't seem to hold a true note.

HUNTING DIARY (excerpt)

September 9, 1971

A Memorable Day

I AWOKE THIS MORNING AT SIX A.M.UNDER AN ALMOST CLEAR SKY. Only a waning sliver of a moon and one lone star still glowed brightly over the ridge of Ruby Mountain. It is cool outside the tent and a light dusting of snow powders the high ridges from the north to the west. It is giving fair warning that the northern summer is preparing to leave this awesome scene. A Whiskey Jack just swooped past where I am sitting on a log next to the cooking fire where I just prepared and ate my breakfast, and am now writing in my diary.

Mr. Jack greeted me with a soft and gentle "tweet" while perched upon a frozen willow twig, cocking his head at me, pleading for a morsel from my breakfast plate. I gave it to him. Now he's cleaning my plate and eats with great urgency. Perhaps he already knows how cold and hungry the long northern winter will be. Perhaps he just worries another bird will steal it from him?

I don't recall exactly how long I sat there by the warm fire, viewing the majestic scenery for signs of life. Now the sun is rising slowly over an as yet unnamed mountain peak, and begins to warm my back. Aside from the sounds of gently rushing waters, the tears of Ruby Creek on my left, and from that other, nameless trickling stream on my right, the world is silent for the moment. With no breeze, the world is as peaceful as an empty church. The smoke from my fire and tobacco pipe spirals straight upwards to fuse with the eternal blue.

Before me, seemingly untouchable, rose the majestic Ruby, with its newly-white ridges that sweep gently to the Northwest. There in the distance they seem to lose their identity in a magnificent mountain panorama. On the lower slopes the autumn colors have become more attractive and frivolously bright with each passing day. I feel as though I'm watching the slow development of A Great Master's colour painting. Around our camp some fireweed is still blooming defiantly, even though its leaves are frosted and dying in a splendor of blood red.

Golden aspen leaves shiver in the still air and flutter onto the cold ground. My fine feathered friend, Jack has finished cleaning my plate. He hopped onto a willow twig and caused a shower of snow-white, fluffy seeds to drift gently to the frozen ground. My world is still silent as I re-light my pipe.

For a week now I have watched a group of Ptarmigan dressing themselves in winter's white. I physically feel in my bones that there will be no time like this ever again in my world. I watched the first shy peak of the rising sun caressing a beautiful, perfectly groomed, tiny tree. Through the rays it glistens akin to a halo on its tiny branches. It's a blue spruce hardly taller than the gopher sitting beside it. Suddenly it sparkles brighter and prettier than big city lights at Christmas time. A fair shadow it casts among its elders... a proud and free shadow it is indeed. It is entitled to cast as large a shadow as it possibly can.

It is now 10:30 a.m. Vancouver time… a great city so very far removed from this beautiful wilderness reality. Sometimes I tend to feel it is too far removed from my reality here. It too, is a wilderness of its own.

Vancouver is not the worst city I've ever known by far. My hunting partners are still sleeping on Vancouver time as well. But for the life of me, I cannot understand why they prefer to sleep away such a beautiful, holy, resurgence of the world.

Is a man's measure of time on this earth surely not short enough already? Just to realize that while one is sleeping here, even the mighty mountains shrink and crumble into dust. A mountain's time on earth is limited, as is mine. Today I can empathize and sympathize with these mountains, and even shed a tear with them. But then, perhaps I'm just getting to be a foolish old man who thinks and feels too much.

Perhaps I'm no longer even a real hunter? Why else do I prefer to sit in the sparkling morning's glory and scribble notes, rather than climb the timbered slopes or bare ridges for a chance at a giant bull moose... or up to the snow fields for a magnificent Osborn caribou bull. Or, go after the awe inspiring old grizzly with the blonde streak of fur along his back. I call him 'Old Yellow-Stripe'? Three times I have spotted him this week, while he is peacefully harvesting the last of an overripe blueberry crop. He is definitely an easy prey for a hunter.

Or, I could be hunting that clever, silver-saddled Stone ram for his amber colored, fully curled, flaring horns? Is he not the hunters' recognized greatest trophy of them all? Yesterday... when I had that ram in my rifle's sights he was innocently grazing with a younger brother... only a single breath away from certain death. I realized suddenly that the ancient, driving urge of my younger self to hunt and kill seems to have left me.

I am not hungry these days. I suppose it was that memorable day on the faraway slopes of another mountain, when I killed a fine California Bighorn ram that started my emotional change. It was so difficult and nerve-racking to hunt him. But it was so very easy to kill him.

I have felt guilty about him ever since. So damn foolishly clever I was at that time, so cunning, so hell-bent on being 'successful' among my peers.

But when this fine ram and noble creature lay crumpled at my feet I would have gladly recalled my bullet. Yes, I still feel the ancient urge to hunt and kill my game quite often so I shall probably kill again. Alas, I'm just as certain that I will suffer remorse for having killed even though now only for food.

In my younger days, when the blood flowed hotter through my veins, the killing part of the hunt was easy. But it seems on the other hand, back in those days, the hunt itself was much more difficult. It required much study, dedication, and hard fieldwork, not to mention a huge monetary commitment. Just to learn how to hunt was often frustrating and difficult. Years passed before I even got to see desirable big game in its natural habitat. Other new hunters I knew quit the chase. But something always drew me back into the mountains, and into the forest, until finally I became a successful hunter.

It is 2 p.m. now. I just returned from a quick hunt for my supper. A flock of blue grouse had landed in a pine tree not far from my camp and with a 12 gauge I went after them. They must've all belonged to a single family, because they didn't scatter when I dropped the first bird. This was peculiar because blue grouse don't normally act like foolhen's.

These birds merely flew to another tree and let me kill two more. I suppose I could have killed the whole bunch, but I felt three birds was enough. We each had one bird for supper! When I returned to camp my partners had finally abandoned their warm soft beds and gone hunting. I cleaned and plucked the birds for the dinner pot, and continued to observe the majestic nature surrounding me.

4 PM. It is a little windy now, but still warm in the tent. I thought I just heard a wolf howl. The sound came from the slope of Ruby Mountain. With my binoculars I tried to spot the animal. No luck! I tried to imitate the howl and to my great surprise the wolf answered me back. I am thrilled!

4:30 PM. No more howls. Perhaps the animal was just trying to tell me how a howl ought to sound. My repeated efforts were ignored. I like to think that my calling is accurate enough, but more than likely Mr. Wolf considers me a joke.

6 PM the sun has already slipped behind the high snowy ridges of yet another faraway mountain. From a distance I hear voices talking. It appears my partners are returning to camp, so it's time to begin cooking our supper. I suppose they'll be doing a lot of yakking about their day tonight and making plans for tomorrow, so there will be little time then for my notes and writing.

But that's alright with me. It's all part of the great outdoor experience. It was a grand day for me out here mostly on my own. I have no complaints.

The Call of the Wild

(My favourite poet)

Robert William Service

Have you gazed on naked grandeur where there's nothing else to gaze on,
Set pieces and drop-curtain scenes galore,
Big mountains heaved to heaven, which the blinding sunsets blazon,
Black canyons where the rapids rip and roar?
Have you swept the visioned valley with the green stream streaking through it,
Searched the Vastness for a something you have lost?
Have you strung your soul to silence? Then for

God's sake go and do it;
Hear the challenge, learn the lesson, pay the cost.

Have you wandered in the wilderness, the sagebrush desolation,
The bunch-grass levels where the cattle graze?
Have you whistled bits of rag-time at the end of all creation,
And learned to know the desert's little ways?
Have you camped upon the foothills, have you galloped o'er the ranges,
Have you roamed the arid sun-lands through and through?
Have you chummed up with the mesa? Do you know its moods and changes?
Then listen to the Wild – it's calling you.

Have you known the Great White Silence, not a snow-gemmed twig aquiver?
(Eternal truths that shame our soothing lies.)

Have you broken trail on snowshoes? mushed your huskies up the river,
Dared the unknown, led the way, and clutched the prize?
Have you marked the map's void spaces, mingled with the mongrel races,
Felt the savage strength of brute in every thew?
And though grim as hell the worst is, can you round it off with curses?
Then hearken to the Wild–it's wanting you.

Have you suffered, starved and triumphed, groveled down, yet grasped at glory,
Grown bigger in the bigness of the whole?

'Done things' just for the doing, letting babblers tell the story,
Seeing through the nice veneer the naked soul?
Have you seen God in His splendors, heard the text that nature renders?
(You'll never hear it in the family pew.)
The simple things, the true things, the silent men who do things—
Then listen to the Wild – it's calling you.

They have cradled you in custom, they have primed you with their preaching,
They have soaked you in convention through and through;
They have put you in a showcase; you're a credit to their teaching—
But can't you hear the Wild? – it's calling you.
Let us probe the silent places, let us seek what luck betide us;
Let us journey to a lonely land I know.
There's a whisper on the night-wind, there's a star agleam to guide us,
And the Wild calling, calling… let us go.

The Cremation of Sam McGee

*There are strange things done in the midnight sun
By the men who moil for gold;
The Arctic trails have their secret tales
That would make your blood run cold;
The Northern Lights have seen queer sights,
But the queerest they ever did see
Was that night on the marge of Lake Lebarge
I cremated Sam McGee.*

Now Sam McGee was from Tennessee, where the cotton blooms and blows.
Why he left his home in the South to roam 'round the Pole, God only knows.

He was always cold, but the land of gold seemed to hold him like a spell;
Though he'd often say in his homely way that he'd "sooner live in hell".

On a Christmas Day we were mushing our way over the Dawson trail.
Talk of your cold! through the parka's fold it stabbed like a driven nail.
If our eyes we'd close, then the lashes froze till sometimes we couldn't see;
It wasn't much fun, but the only one to whimper was Sam McGee.

And that very night, as we lay packed tight in our robes beneath the snow,
And the dogs were fed, and the stars o'erhead were dancing heel and toe,
He turned to me, and "Cap," says he, "I'll cash in this trip, I guess;
And if I do, I'm asking that you won't refuse my last request."

Well, he seemed so low that I couldn't say no; then he says with a sort of moan:
"It's the cursed cold, and it's got right hold till I'm chilled clean through to the bone.
Yet 'tain't being dead — it's my awful dread of the icy grave that pains;
So I want you to swear that, foul or fair, you'll cremate my last remains."

A pal's last need is a thing to heed, so I swore I would not fail;

And we started on at the streak of dawn; but God! he looked ghastly pale.
He crouched on the sleigh, and he raved all day of his home in Tennessee;
And before nightfall a corpse was all that was left of Sam McGee.

There wasn't a breath in that land of death, and I hurried, horror-driven,
With a corpse half hid that I couldn't get rid, because of a promise given;
It was lashed to the sleigh, and it seemed to say: "You may tax your brawn and brains,
But you promised true, and it's up to you to cremate those last remains."

Now a promise made is a debt unpaid, and the trail has its own stern code.
In the days to come, though my lips were dumb, in my heart how I cursed that load.
In the long, long night, by the lone firelight, while the huskies, round in a ring,
Howled out their woes to the homeless snows — O God! how I loathed the thing.

And every day that quiet clay seemed to heavy and heavier grow;
And on I went, though the dogs were spent and the grub was getting low;
The trail was bad, and I felt half mad, but I swore I would not give in;
And I'd often sing to the hateful thing, and it hearkened with a grin.

Till I came to the marge of Lake Lebarge, and a derelict there lay;
It was jammed in the ice, but I saw in a trice it was called the "Alice May".
And I looked at it, and I thought a bit, and I looked at my frozen chum;
Then "Here", said I, with a sudden cry, "is my cre-ma-tor-eum."

Some planks I tore from the cabin floor, and I lit the boiler fire;
Some coal I found that was lying around, and I heaped the fuel higher;
The flames just soared, and the furnace roared — such a blaze you seldom see;
And I burrowed a hole in the glowing coal, and I stuffed in Sam McGee.

Then I made a hike, for I didn't like to hear him sizzle so;
And the heavens scowled, and the huskies howled, and the wind began to blow.
It was icy cold, but the hot sweat rolled down my cheeks, and I don't know why;
And the greasy smoke in an inky cloak went streaking down the sky.

I do not know how long in the snow I wrestled with grisly fear;
But the stars came out and they danced about ere again I ventured near;
I was sick with dread, but I bravely said: "I'll just take a peep inside.
I guess he's cooked, and it's time I looked". . . then the door I opened wide.

And there sat Sam, looking cool and calm, in the heart of the furnace roar;
And he wore a smile you could see a mile, and he said: "Please close that door.
It's fine in here, but I greatly fear you'll let in the cold and storm —
Since I left Plumtree, down in Tennessee, it's the first time I've been warm."

There are strange things done in the midnight sun
By the men who moil for gold;
The Arctic trails have their secret tales
That would make your blood run cold;
The Northern Lights have seen queer sights,
But the queerest they ever did see
Was that night on the marge of Lake Lebarge
I cremated Sam McGee.

PHOTOS

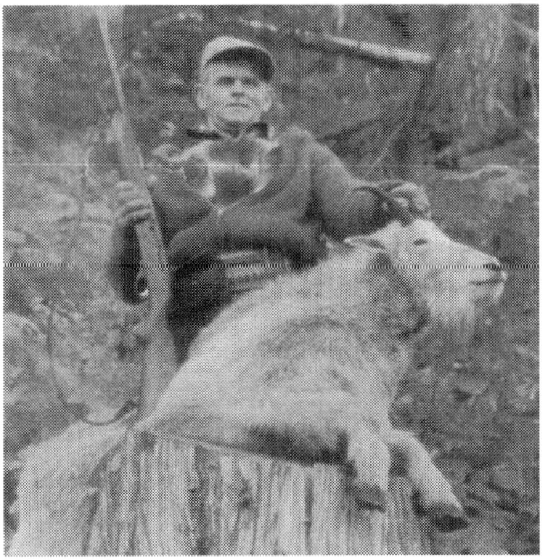

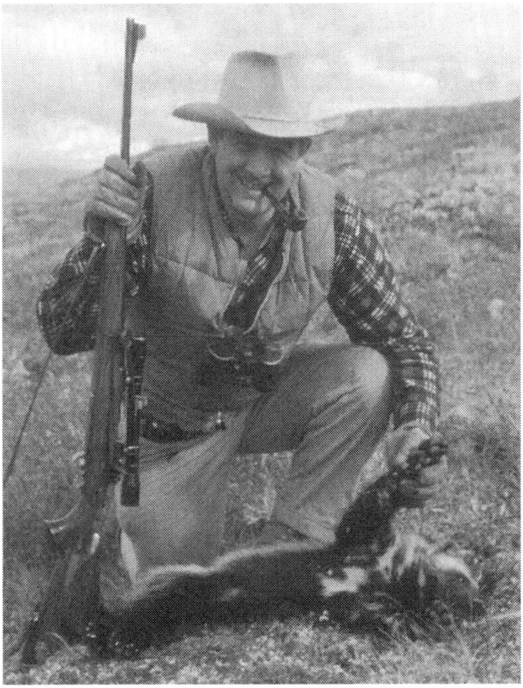

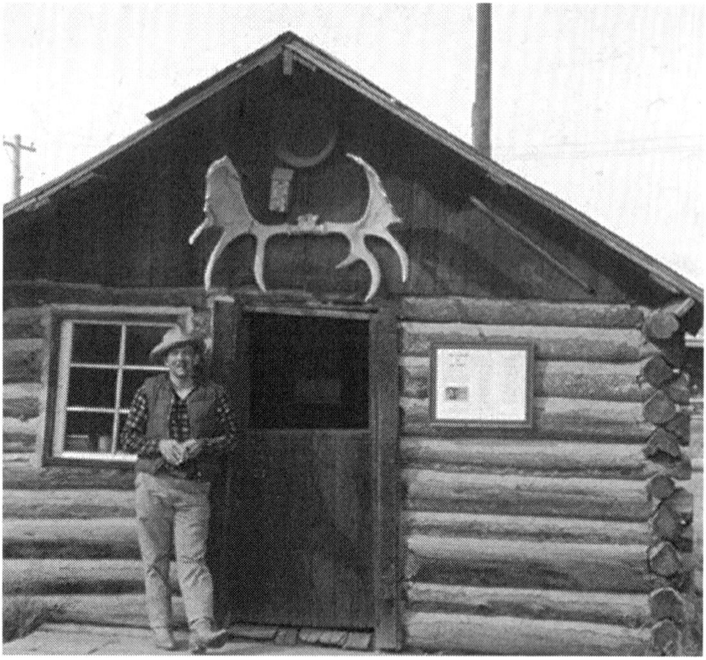

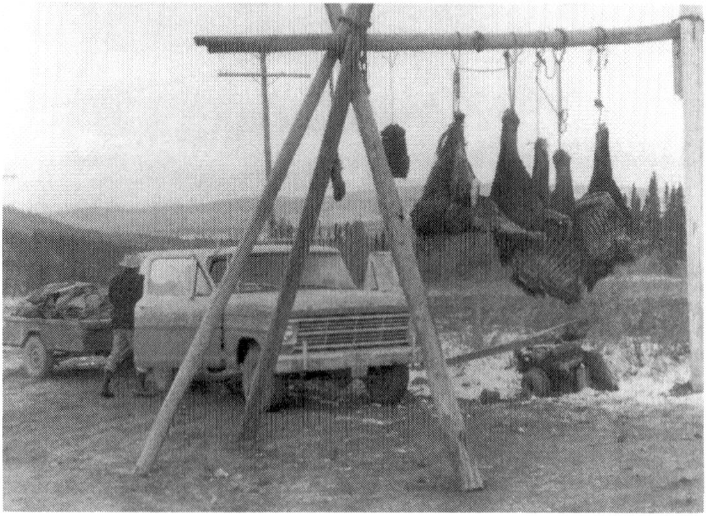

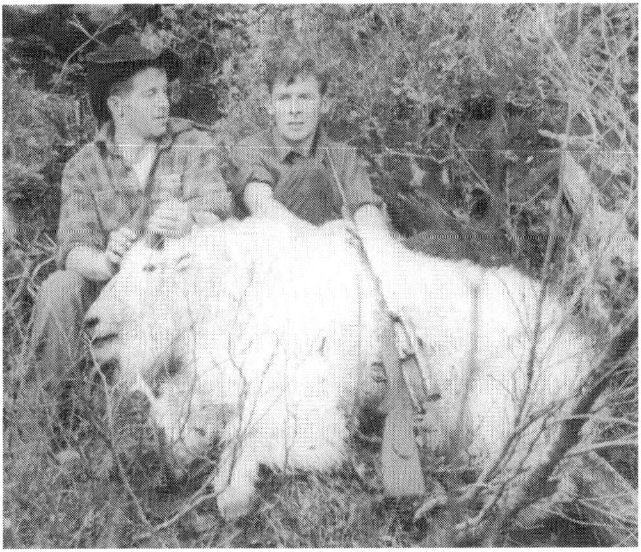

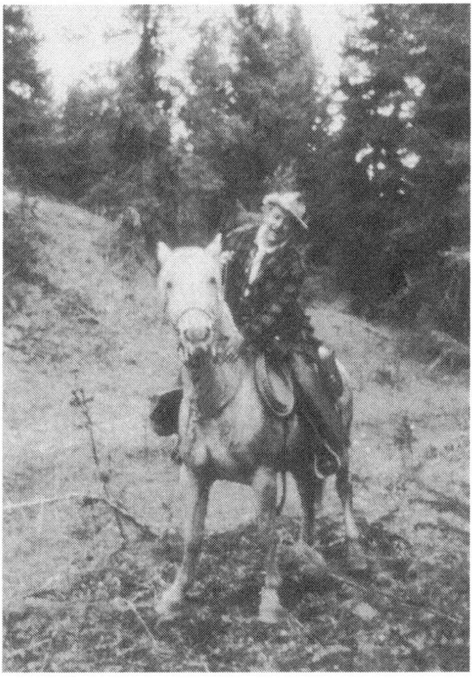

Henry 1951

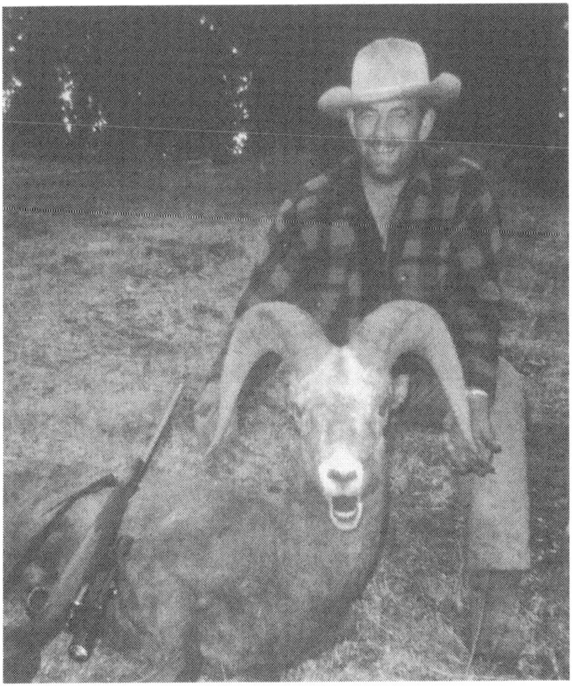

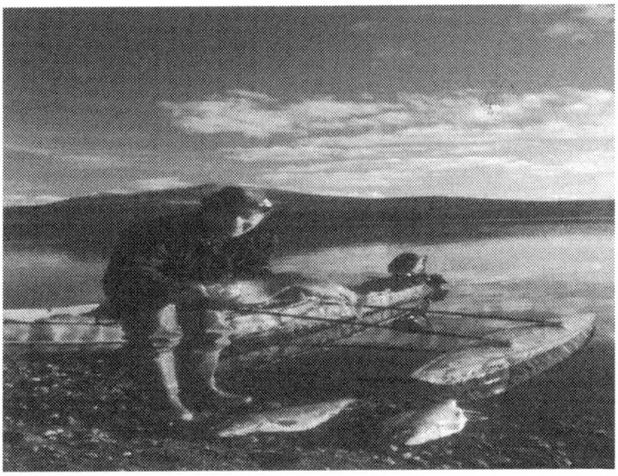

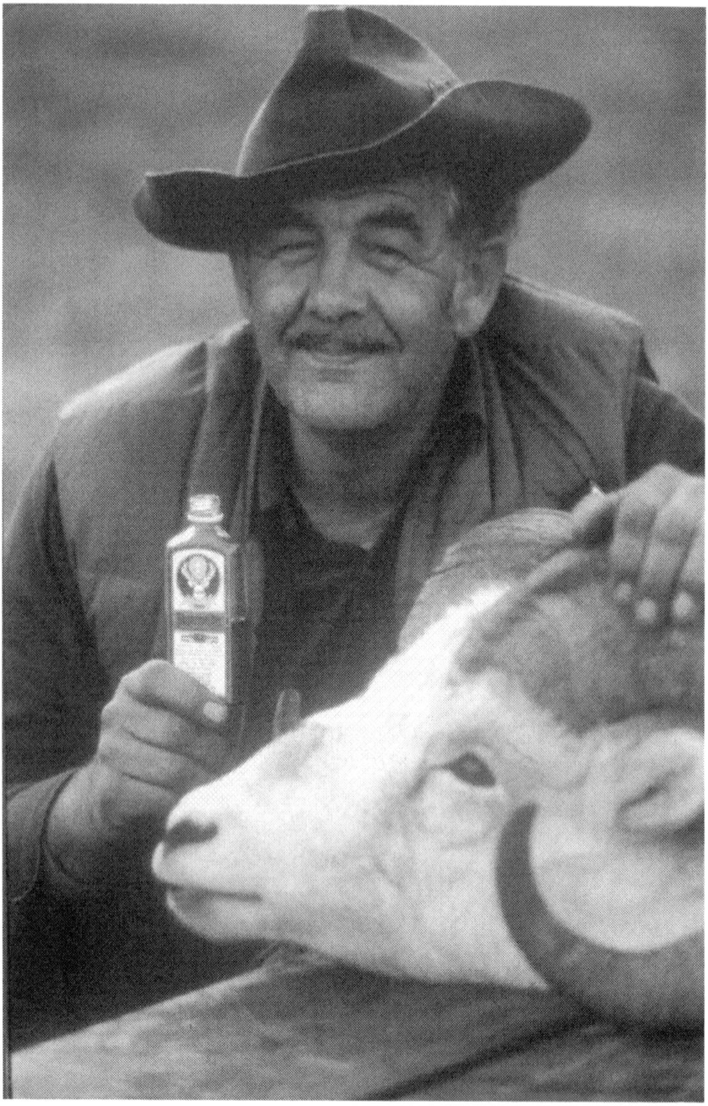

Henry above Atlin Lake and the Llewellyn Glacier in the distance

About Henry

For many years I fought for common-sense controls over those individual and industrial polluters of our Coquitlam River.

I was an active participant:

Port Coquitlam Recreational Council

Port Coquitlam & District Hunting & Fishing Club

B.C. Chapter, Canadian Hemophilia Society

Coquitlam River Water Management Study (Department of the Environment)

****

My daughter, Hella Prante has compiled these stories into book format because I have long gone to the happy hunting grounds up in Atlin B.C. .

She can be reached via email at:

HellaPrante@gmail.com

If you enjoyed these stories Hella will sure appreciate your review on Amazon.

Thanks again.

This is the last of the Great Hunting Adventures series for now.

www.greathuntingadventures.com

Manufactured by Amazon.ca
Bolton, ON